Instant Vortex Air Fryer Oven Cookbook For Beginners

Affordable, Easy, Delicious And Healthy Air Fryer Oven Recipes to Enjoy All the Flavor of Frying for You and Your Family!

by: Robert M Davis

TABLE OF CONTENTS

INTRODUCTION

Air-frying food is a perfect alternative to conventional frying. It needed investment in yet another countertop gadget. No more. Frigidaire launched the first gas, electric, and induction ranges on the market with an air fryer integrated straight into your oven.

Air frying is a cooking process that circulates high-speed hot air in your oven using convection fans. This produces a moist, fried crust with even-browning on all sides using little or no oil compared to conventional deep frying.

Using air-fried is as simple as using your microwave. Second, make sure to preheat the oven to temperature before adding your food.

The air fry feature works better on a single oven rack, which can be programmed between 170°F and 550°F. This allows air to flow around food, making it cooked uniformly and delicious.

Finally, observe the instructions for food preparation, amount, time, and temperature. Learn more about improving your frying experience with these useful tips.

1. BACON AND EGG CUP OF WITH AVOCADO

Prep Time: 10 mins

Cook Time: 20 mins

Servings: 06 Cup

Ingredients

- 6 rashers bacon
- 3 small avocados
- 3 tsp hot sauce or as need
- Salt and pepper
- Squeeze of lemon juice
- 6 Eggs free runs

Instructions

1. Heat the oven to 430F.
2. Line every bacon muffin mold - I used a small piece to lay on the bottom of the pan, then a stretch of bacon to run around the outer side.
3. Place the bacon in the oven for 10-15minutes until crispy.
4. When frying, peel and mash avocados in a bowl. Add hot sauce, lemon juice squeeze, and salt and pepper pinch.
5. Remove the stove bacon. Add mashed avocado to bacon rings using a tsp. The bacon can shrink somewhat, but try filling the bacon middle. Using the spoon back in the center of each mold for the egg to rest in.
6. Crack an egg into each muffin's middle. Return tin to the oven for 10 minutes before the eggs are cooked.
7. When fried, extract from the oven and let them cool slowly. Run a knife through each cup and raise it with a spoon.

Cook's Note

If you use these to cook meals, let the Cups calm full, then pop them in the fridge. Heat them 10 minutes at 360F.

Nutrition Facts

Calories: 316kcal | Carbohydrates: 9g | Protein: 10g | Fat: 28g | Cholesterol: 178mg | S odium: 326mg | Potassium: 592mg | Fiber: 7g | Sugar: 1g | Calcium: 37mg | Iron: 1.4m g

2. BACON & AVOCADO HASH BROWN EGG

Prep Time: 10 mins

Cook Time: 35 mins

Total Time: 45 mins

Ingredients

- 3 1/2 Cups of hash browns thawed
- 3 Tbsp olive oil
- 6 Eggs
- Salt and pepper as need
- 1/2 California Diced Avocado
- 1/2 cup of shredded cheddar cheese
- 6 Slices diced bacon

Instructions

1. Heat the oven to 425ºF. Spray a 12 cups muffin tin with spray and set aside.
2. Pour brown hash into a bowl. If frozen, partially thaw in the microwave for a minute or two. Season 1/2 tsp. Salt, 1/4 tsp. Pepper. Pepper. Add 1 tbsp olive oil swirl until the brown mass is filled.
3. Line each muffin cup with seasoned hash browns, press down to match each cup's bottom and sides, forming crust.
4. Cooking muffins in the oven can take 20 minutes. If the hash browns are mushy on the rim, you can cook a few minutes longer or place a few minutes in the broiler to get golden brown.
5. Lower temperature at 325F. Whisk eggs in a salt & pepper bowl as desired. Fold in cheese, avocado and bacon. In each hash brown crust, scoop egg mixture and place in the oven. Bake 15-20 minutes or until eggs are ready.
6. Let cool for a few minutes, then use a butter knife, scrape each egg Cup's outer rim and remove. Serve, enjoy! Refrigerate all leftovers and serve 45 seconds in the microwave. Even decent room temperature!

3. CINNAMON FRENCH TOAST

Prep Time: 05 mins

Cook Time: 06 mins

Ingredients

- 2 thick slices of brioche bread
- 1 large egg
- 2 tbsps milk
- 1/4 tsp vanilla extract
- 1/4 Cup of granulated sugar
- 1 tsp ground cinnamon
- 2 Tbsp unsalted butter
- 2 tbsp mascarpone
- Maple Syrup
- Fresh Raspberries

Instructions

1. Cut each slice into two triangles.
2. Whisk egg, milk and vanilla extract in a large, shallow bowl.
3. Place sugar and cinnamon on a pan, mix with a fork.
4. Heat butter in a big skillet until bubbling. Dip the egg mixture bread triangles to coat both ends. Don't abandon it when it goes soggy. It's just a brief dip.
5. Place eggy bread in the hot pan. Cook until golden brown. Remove from pan and place in cinnamon sugar. Coat sugar on both ends.
6. Serve toast with mascarpone, maple syrup and new raspberries.

4. BANANA CINNAMON FRENCH TOAST

Prep Time: 05 mins

Cook Time: 20 mins

Ingredients

- 2 slightly overripe bananas
- 4 eggs
- 2 tsp vanilla extract
- 1 tbsp cinnamon
- 1/2 Cup of milk
- 12 slices oatnut

Instructions

1. Place bananas, eggs, vanilla, and cinnamon in a blender.
2. Puree when mixed, and the mixture is mildly frothy.
3. Pour into a bowl to match a slice of bread.
4. Spray a non-stick pan on medium-high.
5. Add a slice of bread into the egg mixture.
6. Place on the skillet, repeat however many slices match.
7. Cook until golden brown, around 2-3 minutes.
8. Repeat with the bread and banana-egg mixture left.
9. You'll enjoy this traditional Banana Cinnamon French Toast Recipe!

Cook's Note

- When dipping, don't saturate the bread: cover it with the custard mixture and place it on a hot skillet. Hearing an intense sizzle!
- To avoid the finished slices of French toast from soggy when cooking the remainder, place them on a rack in the warm oven on a baking sheet.

Nutrition Facts

Calories: 444kcal | Carbohydrates: 71g | Fat: 9g | Protein: 18g |Cholesterol: 166mg | Sodium: 657mg | Potassium: 516mg | Fiber: 6g | Sugar: 16g | Calcium: 223mg | Iron: 4.9mg

---

5. TOMATO ONION OMELETTE

Total Time: 15 - 30 mins

Servings: 04

Ingredients

- 1 Cup of Besan
- 2 Tomato
- 1 Onion
- 1 green chilli
- 1/4 tsp carom seeds
- Ginger
- Coriander leaves
- Oil as needed
- Salt and red chilli powder as need

Instructions

1. Paste the tomato and ginger. Cut onions into small bits.
2. Mix a began paste with tomato and ginger paste. Add chili, coriander and half the chopped onion.
3. Add cinnamon, red chili powder, again seeds and blend well.
4. Heat a non-stick pan and add grease. Pour on the pan about 2 serving spoon paste, spread it thinly and spread some onions.
5. Now let it cook and change side after 3-4 minutes. After cooking another 2 minutes, it's ready to eat.
6. Serve with honey, ketchup and salt. Poor as sandwich stuffing.

6. VEGGIE CRUSTLESS QUICHE

Prep & Cook Time: 20 mins + 20 mins

Servings: 04

Ingredients

- 1 tbsp butter
- 8 ounces thinly sliced cremini mushrooms
- 1 minced shallot
- 2 Cup of loosely packed spinach
- Kosher salt
- Freshly ground black pepper
- 8 large eggs
- 1/4 Cup of whole milk
- 1/4 Cup of oil-packed sun-dried finely chopped tomatoes
- 1/4 Cup of freshly grated Parmesan

Instructions

1. Heat the oven to 375°. Melt butter in a medium-heat skillet. Add mushrooms and cook for 2 minutes, quickly.
2. Cover and cook until mushrooms are soft and golden, 5-6 minutes. Cook shallot until fragrant, 1 minute.
3. Add spinach and simmer for 1 minute more. Season with salt and pepper and fire.
4. Whisk eggs, cream, onions, and parmesan in a large bowl. Fold in mushroom mixture, season with salt and pepper again. When fried, the eggs will be cooked to their final cooking time.
5. Let cool 3 minutes before slicing.

7. TOMATO, SCALLION, AND CHEDDAR FRITTATA

Prep Time: 15 mins

Cook Time: 10 mins

Servings: 06

Ingredients

- 1 tbsp extra virgin olive oil
- 1 bunch thinly sliced scallions
- 2 Cup of grape tomatoes
- Coarse salt and ground pepper
- 8 large lightly beaten eggs
- 1/2 Cup of grated cheddar

Instructions

1. Heat the oven to 425F. Heat oil over medium-high in a 10-inch oven-proof skillet. Add scallions and onions, season with salt and pepper, simmer for 5 minutes.
2. Add eggs, cheese, salt and pepper, and combine. Bake at 400F for about 2 minutes. Set skillet in oven and bake for 10-13 minutes.
3. Invertor slip frittata on a tray, sliced into 6 wedges. Serve warm or room temperature.

Cook's Note

The frittata tends to be more liquid when moved to the oven, but as long as the edges are set, the eggs cook uniformly.

8. AMERICAN FRITTATA

Prep Time: 15 mins

Cook Time: 15 mins

Servings: 08

Ingredients

- 4 peeled and cubed potatoes
- ½ sliced onions
- 1 tbsp vegetable oil
- 8 beaten eggs
- ¾ Cup of cubed ham
- Salt and pepper as need
- ¾ Cup of shredded Cheddar cheese

Instructions

1. Bring a big salted water boil. Cook potatoes until soft but solid, about 5 minutes. Drain and cool aside. Meanwhile, heat to 350F.
2. Heat oil medium in a cast-iron skillet. Add onions and cook gently, occasionally stirring, until tender.
3. Drain eggs, rice, sausage, salt, and pepper. Cook until eggs are firm down, about 5 minutes. Top frittata with shredded cheese and place in a preheated oven until cheese is melted and eggs are fully strong.

Nutrition Facts

234 calories: protein 12.4g: carbohydrates 20.8g: fat 11.4g: cholesterol 203.4mg: sodium 298.4mg

9. DELUXE BACON ONION OMELET

Prep Time: 15 mins

Cook Time: 20 mins

Servings: 02

Ingredients

- 4 slices bacon
- 3 eggs
- 1 tsp water
- Cooking spray
- 1 tbsp butter
- ½ diced white onion

Instructions

1. Heat the oven to 375F. Arrange baking sheet bacon.
2. Bake 10-12 minutes in the preheated oven until crisp.
3. Beat eggs and water in a bowl.
4. Cool the bacon on paper towels, maybe 5 minutes. Cut into bits
5. Spray a 10-inch non-stick skillet with spray. Melt butter over medium heat, around 2 minutes. Add onion before butter finishes foaming. Cook and stir until browned, 4 to 5 minutes.
6. Increase medium-high heat. Pour eggs into the skillet and steam for about 2 minutes. Raise the omelet with a spatula as the center rises: tip the skillet to the center of the plate. Cook till set, 2-4 minutes. Sprinkle bacon on the omelet and fold in half with the spatula.

Cook's Note

Cut the omelet in half for better maneuvering before serving.

Nutrition Facts

259 calories: protein 15.5g: carbohydrates 6.1g: fat 19.3g: cholesterol 310.2mg: sodium 485mg

10. SHARON'S EGG AND HAM SCRAMBLE

Prep Time: 10 mins

Cook Time: 10 mins

Servings: 04

Ingredients

- 8 beaten eggs
- 3 tbsp milk
- ¼ tsp seasoned salt
- Salt and ground black pepper as need
- ¼ Cup of olive oil
- 1 jalapeno seeded and minced pepper
- ½ Cup of chopped deli slices Applewood smoked ham
- 1 Cup of finely shredded divided Cheddar cheese

Instructions

1. In a bowl, beat eggs, sugar, seasoned garlic, salt, and black pepper.
2. Heat olive oil over medium-high in a large non-stick skillet: saute jalapeno in hot oil until slightly softened, 2-3 minutes. Add ham to jalapeno, cook until heated, around 1 minute.
3. Pour the paste into ham. Cook and stir until eggs are dry, 3 to 5 minutes. Sprinkle 1/2 of Cheddar cheese over eggs: boil and stir until melted. Transfer eggs to a plate and sprinkle the remaining cheese.

Nutrition Facts

400 calories: protein 23.1g: carbohydrates 1.9g: fat 33.7g: cholesterol 411mg: sodium 625.2mg.

11. CHEESY HAM AND EGG IN A HOLE BAKE

Prep Time: 05 mins

Cook Time: 15 mins

Serves Makes: 04

Ingredients

- 4 slices bread
- Butter, as needed
- 4 slices ham
- 4 eggs
- 1/ 2 Cup of shredded cheese
- Salt and black pepper, As need
- Scallions, Chives or chopped for garnish

Instructions

1. Heat the oven to 350ºF. Line a parchment-paper baking sheet. Lay bread slices on the pan and press each slice with a measuring cup to make a divot.
2. Butter toast's sides. Place a ham in the divot center and crack an egg inside. Sprinkle bread's buttered sides with shredded cheese. Salt and pepper season.
3. Bake 15 minutes or before you like the egg. Sprinkle with chips/scallions15.

12. CHICKEN OMELETTE

Prep & Cook Time: 31-40 mins + 11-15 mins

Servings: 04

Ingredients

- Boneless chicken boiled and shredded 200 grams
- Salt as need & 6 Eggs
- Black peppercorns crushed as need
- 1 tsp Red chilli powder
- 1 tsp Chaat masala
- 1 sliced medium onion
- 2 tbsp Spring onion greens chopped
- 1/2 Cup of Milk
- 2 tbsp Butter & 2 tbsp Oil
- 8 slices white bread

Instructions

1. Mix half the chicken, 3 eggs, salt, broken peppercorns, 1/2 tsp chili powder, 1/2 tsp chaat masala, half the onion and 1 tbsp spring onion greens in a bowl. Add 1/4 cup and blend well.
2. Heat oil in a non-stick Tawa. Pour on and scatter the formulated mixture. Dip egg slices of bread and set aside. Cook before browned omelet underside.
3. Place 2 slices of bread side-by-side in the omelet centre, turn and fold the omelet from the ends.
4. Place the remaining bread slices on top, half, flip and cook until well toasted on both sides. Make 2 or more omelets equally.
5. Serve hot with ketchup.

13. SWEET POTATO HASH WITH EGGS

Prep Time: 10 mins

Cook Time: 20 mins

Servings: 04

Ingredients

- 2 tbsp extra-virgin olive oil
- 1 Cup of red onion
- 2 pounds washed and skin-on sweet potato
- ½ Cup of red bell pepper
- ½ Cup of green bell pepper
- 1 tbsp minced garlic
- ¼ tsp smoked paprika
- Sea salt, as needed for seasoning
- Black pepper, as needed for seasoning
- 4 large eggs
- 1 tbsp thinly sliced green onions

Instructions

1. Heat the oven to 425°F.
2. Heat a big, oven-proof skillet like cast iron over medium heat.
3. Add 2 tbsp. of olive oil, red onions once heated, saute 1 minute.
4. Add garlic, saute 1 minute.
5. Add sweet potatoes, 1/2 tsp salt and 1/4 tsp black pepper, stir, and allow the potatoes to cook unmoved to brown the surface gently, 4 minutes. Stir and saute until soft, 4-6 minutes.

6. Add peppers and saute 2 minutes. Turn off heat, add paprika and mix to blend.
7. Place the eggs in various positions, allowing enough space for them to hatch.
8. The eggs will set when the pan is shook and the yolks will turn brown when shaken, about 7 or 8 minutes.
9. Add from the oven and garnish with green onions, salt and pepper if needed.

14. CINNAMON ROLLS

Prep & Cook Time: 30 mins + 30 mins

Rising time: 02 hrs

Serves: 12

Ingredients

For the Yeast:

- ½ cup of warm water
- 1 package active dry yeast
- 1 tsp cane sugar

Dough:

- ⅓ cup of melted coconut oil
- ½ cup of almond milk
- ⅓ cup of cane sugar
- 1 tsp sea salt
- 2¾ cups of all-purpose flour
- ½ cup of brown sugar
- 1½ tbsp cinnamon

Glaze:

- 1½ cups of sifted powdered sugar
- 3 to 4 tbsp almond milk
- ½ tsp vanilla extract

Instructions

1. Grease a baking dish that is 8x11 or 9x13-inch.
2. Stir together the water, yeast, and sugar in a small bowl. Set aside for 5 mins, or until it is foamy with yeast.
3. Make the dough: Mix the coconut oil, almond milk, sugar, and salt in a medium bowl. Stir in a blend of yeast. In a bowl place the flour, then add the yeast and whisk mixture to combine.
4. It'll be messy with the mixture. Use your fingertips to loosely knead the mixture, then turn it onto a floured board. Knead until smooth for 3 to 4 mins, sprinkle with more flour if necessary, and form into a ball.
5. Brush the coconut oil in a wide bowl and place the dough inside. Cover with plastic wrap and set aside for around 1 hour, in a warm position to grow until doubled in size.
6. Make the filling: In bowl, add the brown sugar and cinnamon.
7. Punch the dough down & stretch it out into a 20x14-inch rectangle on a floured board. Brush with 2 tbsp of molten coconut oil and dust within 1/2 inch of the cinnamon sugar edges.
8. Roll tightly into a log, then cut into 12 rolls, starting at one of the 14-inch narrow ends. Place the rolls cut-side-up, cover, and let rise for 1 hour in the baking dish.
9. Heat the oven to 350°F.
10. Make the glaze: whisk the powdered sugar, 3 tablespoons of almond milk, and vanilla together in a medium bowl until smooth. When it's too thick, add more almond milk.
11. Cook the rolls for 25 to 30 minutes or until the surface is mildly golden. Remove and allow 10 mins to cool, then drizzle on top of the glaze and serve.

15. CLASSIC FRENCH TOAST

Prep Time: 06 mins

Cook Time: 16 mins

Serves: 04

Ingredients

Macerated Berries:

- 2 cups of diced strawberries
- ½ cup of frozen raspberries, thawed, with their juices
- Pinches of cane sugar

French Toast:

- 4 eggs
- 1 cup of almond milk
- 1 tsp cinnamon
- ¼ tsp cardamom
- Pinch of sea salt
- 8 1-inch slices challah bread
- Coconut oil for brushing
- Maple syrup, for serving

Instructions

1. Make the macerated berries: Mix the strawberries, raspberries, and a few pinches of sugar in a medium bowl. Set aside for the berries to soften for 10 mins. Before eating, stir.
2. Make French toast: Whisk the eggs, milk, cinnamon, cardamom, and salt together in a big dish. In the mixture, dip each slice of bread and set aside the soaked bread on a large tray or plate.
3. Heat a medium-hot non-stick skillet and spray it with coconut oil. Add the slices of bread and cook until golden brown, about 2 minutes on either side. To cook thoroughly without burning, reduce the heat to a minimum, as needed. Serve with maple syrup and berries that are macerated.

16. HEALTHY BANANA BREAD

Prep Time: 10 mins

Cook Time: 45 mins

Serves: 08

Ingredients

- 2 mashed ripe bananas
- ½ cup of coconut sugar
- ¾ cup of almond milk
- ⅓ cup of extra-virgin olive oil
- 1 tsp vanilla extract
- 1 tsp apple cider vinegar
- 1 ½ cups of whole wheat pastry flour
- ½ cup of almond flour
- 2 tsp baking powder
- ¼ tsp baking soda
- ½ tsp sea salt
- ½ tsp cinnamon
- ¼ tsp nutmeg
- ½ cup of chopped walnuts topping
- 2 tbsp chopped walnuts
- 1 1/2 tbsp rolled oats

Instructions

1. Heat the oven to 350°F. Brush some olive oil with a 9x5-inch loaf pan.
2. Mix the mashed bananas with butter, almond milk, olive oil, vanilla, and apple cider vinegar in a big bowl and whisk until mixed.
3. Combine the flour, salt, baking soda, cinnamon,baking powder, and nutmeg in a medium bowl.
4. For the wet ingredients, add the dry ingredients to the bowl and stir until just mixed, then mix in the walnuts. Pour the diced walnuts and the oats into the prepared pan and sprinkle with them.
5. Bake for 42 to 50 mins, or until the middle of the toothpick comes out clean.

Cook's Note

I like Whole Wheat Pasty Flour from Bob's Red Mill because it's lighter than standard wheat flour. A 50/50 blend of standard whole wheat flour and all-purpose flour may also be used.

17. BLUEBERRY BAKED OATMEAL

Prep Time: 10 mins

Cook Time: 50 mins

Serves: 08

Ingredients

- 2 tbsp ground flaxseed
- 6 tbsp warm water
- 2 cups of whole rolled oats
- ½ cup of slivered almonds
- ½ cup of hemp seeds
- ⅔ cup of coconut flakes
- 1/4 cup of brown sugar
- 1 tsp baking powder
- 1 tsp cinnamon
- ¾ tsp sea salt
- ¾ cup of almond milk
- 1/4 cup of maple syrup
- 3 tbsp melted coconut oil
- 1 chopped banana
- 1 cup of sliced strawberries
- ½ cup of blueberries

Instructions

1. Heat the oven to 350°F. Using cooking spray to spray an 8x8-inch baking dish.
2. In a bowl, mix the flaxseed & warm water and set it aside for around 5 mins to thicken.
3. Reserve and set aside 2 teaspoons of the nuts, hemp seeds, and coconut flakes. Combine the peas, remaining almonds, hemp seeds, and flakes of coconut, and the baking powder, cinnamon, salt, and brown sugar in a large bowl.
4. Mix the almond milk, maple syrup, and coconut oil in a medium bowl and whisk to combine. Stir in the mixture of flaxseed and combine until smooth.
5. Pour the wet ingredients into the dry bowl and mix to blend.
6. In the baking bowl, layer the bananas and strawberries and add the oat mixture on top. Sprinkle the reserved almonds, hemp seeds, and coconut flakes with the blueberries.
7. Bake for 40-50 mins or until the middle is set and the top is crisp. I find it best to wedge a knife in to make sure that the middle is neatly thickened. Before serving, detach and let cool for 15 mins.

Cook's Note

In this recipe, if you want to reduce the sugar, avoid the brown sugar and substitute 1/3 cup maple syrup.

18. COCONUT MANGO MUFFINS

Serves: 12 Muffins

Ingredients

- 1 tbsp ground flaxseed
- 3 tbsp water
- 2 tsp fresh lime juice
- ¾ cup of Almond Breeze Almondmilk Coconutmilk
- 2 cups of spelt flour
- 2 tsp baking powder
- ½ tsp salt
- ½ tsp cinnamon
- ½ cup of cane sugar
- 2 tbsp sugar for the topping
- ¼ cup of melted unrefined coconut oil
- 1 tsp vanilla
- 1 cup of finely diced ripe mango
- ½ to ¾ cup of unsweetened coconut flakes

Instructions

1. Heat the oven to 350°F. Line the paper liners with a 12-cup muffin tin.
2. To thicken, mix the ground flaxseed and water and set aside. Stir in the almond milk with the lime juice and set aside.
3. Combine the flour, baking powder, salt, cinnamon, and 1/2 cup of sugar in a large bowl. Whisk the flaxseed mixture, almond milk/lime juice mixture, coconut oil, and vanilla together in a medium bowl.
4. Onto bowl of dry ingredients, pour the wet ingredients, and stir until just mixed. Do not overregulate. Fold the diced mango in.
5. Divide the mixture uniformly into muffin cups, filling about three-quarters of each one with the batter. Sprinkle with the flakes of coconut and bake for 15 to 20 minutes, or until the inserted toothpick comes out clean. Sprinkle gently with the remaining sugar if necessary. Cool for 10 mins, then place to finish cooling on a wire rack.

19. PISTACHIO GOJI BERRY GRANOLA

Serves: about 02 Cups

Ingredients

- 1 cup of rolled oats
- ½ tsp salt
- 1 tbsp coconut oil
- 3 tbsp maple syrup
- ⅓ cup of chopped pistachios
- ¼ cup of coconut flakes
- 1 tsp cinnamon
- ⅓ cup of goji berries

Instructions

1. Heat a large skillet over low heat on the stove. Then add the oats and scatter them in the pan into a thin layer. For a minute or two, let them start to toast.
2. Add the coconut oil and salt, then mix to blend. For 5-7 min or so, continue to toast the oats, stirring only periodically.
3. Add 1 tbsp of maple syrup at a time, then stir to coat.
4. Add the pistachios, coconut chips, and cinnamon after the oats look pretty toasty. Continue to cook slowly until the coconut flakes and pistachios are toasted but not charred.
5. See closely, when the bottom layer continues to toast, stop and stir it again so that it toasts equally.
6. Remove and stir in the goji berries from the container.
7. Let it cool and enjoy your yogurt as a snack or on top of it.

Cook's Note

I. Be sure to use oats that are registered gluten-free if you're gluten-free.
II. I prefer cooking it in batches so that the Ingredients match in a thin layer in your big skillet to double this recipe. You'll want to toast all evenly.
III. I used a nonstick skillet since it is my main one - if you have cast iron, you will need to change the cooking time.

20. BEST BREAKFAST BURRITO

Prep Time: 15 mins

Cook Time: 30 mins

Serves: 03 to 06

Ingredients

- 1 pound small round yellow potatoes
- Extra-virgin olive oil
- ½ tsp smoked paprika
- Pinches of red pepper flakes
- 1 red bell pepper
- 9 large eggs
- 3 12-inch tortillas
- 1 cup of fresh spinach
- ½ cup of shredded red cabbage
- ½ cup of pico de gallo
- 1 ripe avocado
- ¾ cup of cooked black beans drained
- ½ cup of cilantro leaves
- Sea salt and freshly ground black pepper
- 1 lime, for squeezing
- Cilantro Lime Dressing

Instructions

1. Heat the oven to 425°F. Line the parchment paper with a large baking sheet. On the mat, place the potatoes, drizzle with olive oil, and generously sprinkle with salt and pepper, smoked paprika, and pinches of red pepper flakes. Toss to coat, scatter uniformly over the pan, and bake for 30 minutes or until the sides are golden brown and crisp.
2. Heat the grill pan to low heat on the burner. Place the red pepper on the pan & let it char for 5 minutes on each side, or until the pepper is soft and black grill marks are on each side. Alternatively, you can roast it until soft in the oven. Remove the stem and the ribbing from the pan, and cut the pepper into strips.
3. Scramble the eggs: gently spray a medium nonstick skillet with olive oil and bring it to medium pressure. Add the eggs, and cook them for a few seconds, then stir and scramble until the eggs are ready.
4. Assemble the burritos: divide, if used, between the tortillas, the spinach leaves, and red cabbage. Garnish with eggs, slices of red pepper, black beans, pico de gallo, rice, cilantro, and avocado. Sprinkle with a squeeze of salt and pepper and lime.

5. Over the filling, fold the left and right sides of the tortilla. When the burrito is rolled, fold the bottom flap of the burrito up and over the filling, tuck the sides and the filling. For dipping, wrap in foil, slice, and serve with Cilantro Lime Dressing.

Cook's Note

To prepare these burritos beforehand, I recommend covering them in foil and storing them in the fridge for 1 to 2 days. Or better still, when you're preparing to eat, make the components in advance and wrap them. I don't like frozen/thawed eggs personally, so I don't recommend freezing those eggs.

21. HEALTHY BREAKFAST CASSEROLE

Prep Time: 15 mins

Cook Time: 01 hr 15 mins

Serves: 10 to 12

Ingredients

- 2 cubed sweet potatoes
- 10 to 12 ounces mixed mushrooms
- 1 bunch asparagus, tender parts, chopped
- Extra-virgin olive oil
- 12 large eggs
- ½ cup of almond milk
- 1 minced garlic clove
- ½ to 1 tsp sea salt
- ½ tsp black pepper
- 4 ounces crumbled feta cheese
- 1 chopped bunch of scallions
- 1 cup of thawed frozen peas

Instructions

1. Heat the oven to 400°F. Line 2 parchment paper baking sheets. Using one baking sheet to spread the sweet potatoes, then spread the mushrooms and asparagus on the other baking sheet.
2. Sprinkle with flour, olive oil and pepper, and blend with a pinch of salt and pepper to fill with salt and pepper. For 30 mins, roast the sweet potatoes. In the final 10 mins, place the baking sheet with the mushrooms and asparagus in the oven to roast.

3. Whisk together the eggs, milk, garlic, cinnamon, and black pepper in a medium bowl.
4. Decrease the temperature of the oven to 350°F. Spread a 9x13-inch baking dish gently with nonstick paint. Locate all the sweet potatoes evenly at the bottom of the baking bowl. From the second baking sheet, add half of the vegetables and spread out uniformly. Sprinkle the cheese, scallions, and peas with the feta.
5. Pour generously over the vegetables with the egg mixture. Add the remaining asparagus and mushrooms.
6. Bake until the eggs are set and the sides are softly golden brown, or for 40 to 45 minutes. Before slicing, let the casserole rest for 10 mins.
7. Garnish the microgreens with slices and season with extra salt and pepper, if desired.

Cook's Note

If the feta cheese is used, use 1/2 tsp salt; if the feta cheese is omitted, use 1 tsp salt. The recipe fits into a standard 9x13 plate, even though the pan in the illustration is a bit smaller than a 9x13 pan. You will need to use many pans if you are using a smaller pan.

22. STRAWBERRY SALAD WITH BALSAMIC

Prep Time: 10 mins

Cook Time: 10 mins

Serves: 04

Ingredients

- ¼ cup of balsamic vinegar
- 1 cup of sliced strawberries
- 1 cup of halved cherry tomatoes
- 1 cup of halved mini mozzarella balls
- 1 pitted and diced ripe avocado
- ⅓ cup of toasted pecans
- ⅓ cup of loosely packed basil
- Extra-virgin olive oil
- Sea salt and freshly ground black pepper

Instructions

1. Bring the balsamic vinegar to a high boil over medium heat in a small saucepan. Stir, then raise the heat to low and boil until the vinegar has thickened and halved for around 8 to 10 minutes. Set aside to cool.
2. In a shallow bowl or platter, place the strawberries, cherry tomatoes, mozzarella, avocado, pecans, and basil.
3. Spread olive oil and season with salt and pepper generously. Toss gently. Drizzle with balsamic reduction.

---

23. CREAMY AVOCADO SMOOTHIE

Prep Time: 05 mins

Total Time: 05 mins

Serves: 02 to 03

Ingredients

- 1/2 cup of cubed frozen pineapple
- 2 cups of packed fresh spinach
- 1 ripe avocado
- 1 frozen banana
- 3/4 cup of light coconut milk, canned or from a carton
- 3 tbsp fresh lime juice, + 1/2 tsp zest
- 1 tsp maple syrup
- Pinch of sea salt
- 8 ice cubes

Instructions

1. In a blender, combine pineapple, spinach, avocado, banana, coconut milk, lime juice, maple syrup, salt, ice cubes, and protein powder. Blend until they're creamy.
2. Taste the sweetness to your liking and adjust it. Add more maple syrup if you prefer a sweeter smoothie.
3. Add more coconut milk and blend again if the consistency is too thick.

Cook's Note

I like Aloha Vanilla Plant-Based Protein and Whole Foods French Vanilla Plant Protein.

24. CLASSIC MARGARITA

Prep Time: 05 mins

Total Time: 05 mins

Serves: 01

Ingredients

- 1-ounce tequila
- 1 ounce Cointreau
- 1-ounce fresh lime juice, + lime slices for garnish
- ½ ounce agave nectar, as need
- Sea salt, for the rim

Instructions

1. Salt the bottom of the bottle by rubbing a lime wedge across the lip and dipping it on a small salt platter.
2. In the glass, combine the tequila, Cointreau, and lime juice and fill the rest of the glass with crushed ice.
3. Stir and add to sweeten the agave nectar, if desired. If it's too strong, wait a bit until after the ice melts.

1. MAPLE MUSTARD CHICKEN THIGHS

Prep & Cook Time: 10 mins + 45 mins

Yield: 2 to 4 Servings

Ingredients

- 4 large skins removed bone-in chicken thighs
- 2 tbsp grainy french mustard
- 2 tbsp dijon mustard
- 1 clove minced garlic
- 1/2 tsp dried marjoram
- 2 tbsp maple syrup

Instructions

1. Heat the oven to 375F.
2. Rinse chicken, dry pat. Mix mustard, garlic, marjoram and maple syrup in a bowl.
3. Spread about 1 1/2 tbsp of mustard mixture thinly on top of each chicken leg, be sure to cover as much surface as possible to make a "crust."
4. Bake for 45 to 50 minutes or until the mustard mixture has formed a crust and has been partially hardened.

2. BACON AND CHEESE QUICHE

Prep & Cook Time: 10 mins + 55 mins

Servings: 08

Ingredients

- 1 Pillsbury refrigerated softened pie crust
- 1 Cup of milk & 1 tbsp chopped onion
- 4 slightly beaten eggs
- ¼ tsp salt & ¼ tsp pepper
- 8 slices bacon, crisply cooked, crumbled
- 1 Cup of shredded Swiss or Cheddar cheese
- 1/4 Cup of grated Parmesan cheese

Instructions

1. Heat the oven to 350°F. Place crust in 9-inch pie plate and cover with pie.
2. Mix half-and-a-half, eggs, salt and pepper: set aside. Layer sausage, cheeses and crust-lined plate onion. Pour over egg mixture.
3. Bake 40-50 minutes or until the focused knife comes out clean. Let stand 5 minutes: cut wedges.

Nutrition Facts

Calories420, Total Fat28g, Cholesterol150mg, Sodium600mg, Potassium130mg, Total Carbohydrate29g, Protein12g

---

3. CRISPY KOREAN BBQ CHICKEN WINGS

Prep Time: 10 mins

Cook Time: 40 mins

Additional Time: 01 Hr

Servings: 6 to 8

Ingredients

- 4 pounds chicken wings, broken down into drummettes and flats
- 1/3 Cup of Korean red chili pepper paste
- 1/4 Cup of brown sugar
- 1/4 Cup of soy sauce
- 2 tbsp water
- 1 tbsp sesame oil
- 1 tbsp rice wine vinegar
- 4 minced cloves Garlic
- 1 1/2 tbsp. minced & peeled fresh ginger
- 1 tsp kosher salt
- 1 tsp black pepper
- Garnish: sesame seed, sliced green onion

Instructions

1. Add raw chicken wings to a Ziploc bag.
2. Mix the brown sugar, chili paste, soy sauce, sesame oil, rice wine vinegar, garlic, ginger, salt, and pepper. Add the marinade to the container. Refrigerate at least one Hr.
3. Heat the grill to 400 degrees Fahrenheit until preparing to fire.
4. Connect wings to the grill and cook until skin is crispy and cooked through, alternating every 10-15 minutes. It'll take about 30-40 minutes. They can record 165 UFF on a meat thermometer.
5. When fried, remove wings from the grill and set them aside on a tray.
6. Pour marinade into a saucepan on the grill. Boil the sauce over high heat and boil 1 to 2 minutes, stirring constantly.
7. Dust the completed sauce wings. Garnish with sesame seeds and onion. Serve quickly.

Cook's Note

Follow the wings marinating formula instructions. Heat the oven to 400F to roast the wings. Line a broad parchment-paper rimmed baking sheet.

Spread wings uniformly on the prepared baking dish. Bake 40-60 minutes. No need to turn them halfway, just bake until cooked and crispy.

---

4. BBQ CHICKEN WINGS

Prep Time: 20 mins

Cook Time: 55 mins

Total Time: 01 Hr 15 mins

Ingredients

- 1 1/4 pounds chicken wings
- 2 tbsp oil
- 1/2 tsp salt
- 1 tsp garlic powder
- 1 tsp smoked paprika
- 1/2 tsp black pepper
- BBQ Sauce
- 1 Cup of barbecue sauce
- 1/4 Cup of honey
- 2 tbsp ketchup or hot sauce

Instructions

1. Heat the oven to 425F. Line a parchment sheet and place an oven rack on top.
2. Add the chicken wings in a wide tub, add oil, and flip. Combine salt with garlic powder, dried paprika and black pepper. Add the paste over the chicken wings and coat uniformly.
3. Arrange the seasoned chicken wings in one layer.
4. Bake 40-45 minutes, depending on their height, flipping once after 20 minutes.
5. When baking, wings prepare the sauce.
6. Place honey and hot sauce in a small sauce barbecue sauce. Simmer 2-3 minutes over low heat.
7. Remove the wings and spray with barbecue sauce
8. Bake for 10-15 minutes until glazed and caramelized.
9. Garnish with green onion and serve your favorite sauce. Enjoy it.

Nutrition Facts

Calories:698, Fat:45.2g, Carbohydrates:31g, Sugar: 24.7g, Fiber:0.8g, Protein:42.8g, Cholesterol:179mg, Sodium 1287mg, Calcium 12mg, Iron 1mg, Potassium 162mg.

5. BAKED CHICKEN NUGGETS

Prep Time: 20 mins

Cook Time: 20 mins

Total Time: 40 mins

Ingredients

- 3 skinless & boneless chicken breasts
- 1 Cup of Italian seasoned bread crumbs
- ½ Cup of grated parmesan cheese
- 1 tsp salt
- 1 tsp dried thyme
- 1 tbsp dried basil
- ½ Cup of melted butter

Instructions

1. Heat the oven to 400F.
2. Cut breasts into 1 1/2-inch bits. In a medium bowl, mix crumbs, cheese, cinnamon, thyme and basil. Ok, blend. Place butter in a bowl or dish for dipping.
3. First dip chicken parts into the molten butter, then coat with breadcrumb mixture.
4. Place well-coated chicken parts on a lightly greased baking sheet in one layer and bake 20 minutes in the preheated oven.

Nutrition Facts

308 calories: protein 19.3g: carbohydrates 14.6g: fat 19.1g: cholesterol 81mg: sodium 989mg.

6. REAL CHICKEN NUGGETS WITH SMOKY BBQ SAUCE

Prep Time: 20 mins

Cook Time: 10 mins

Total Time: 30 mins

Ingredients

- 2 tbsp. Mayonnaise
- 2 skinless chicken breast fillets
- 25g fresh breadcrumb
- 25g lightly crushed Weetabix
- Chips or salad , to serve

For the BBQ Sauce:

- 25g light muscovado sugar
- 2 tbsp wine vinegar
- 4 tbsp tomato ketchup
- 1 tbsp Worcestershire sauce
- ¼ tsp smoked paprika

Instructions

1. Heat the oven to 220C. Marinate for 30 minutes or overnight, then add both ingredients into the meat.
2. Meanwhile, place mayonnaise in a chicken bowl and stir well to coat.

3. Mix crumbs with Weetabix with seasoning. Using crumbs to coat the chicken on a pan.
4. Spread chicken parts on a baking tray and bake for 10 minutes until soft but juicy. Serve with BBQ and chips or salad.

---

7. LASAGNA DIP

Prep Time: 10 mins

Cook Time: 23 mins

Total Time: 33 mins

Ingredients

- 1 1/2 Cup of Italian sausage
- 6 oz softened cream cheese
- 4 oz ricotta
- 3 Cup of shredded mozzarella
- 1/2 Cup of shredded parmesan
- 1/2 Cup of marinara sauce
- 2 tsp Italian seasoning
- 1 tsp garlic powder
- Salt and pepper, as need
- Fresh parsley for garnish
- 1 baguette

Instructions

1. Heat the oven to 350F.
2. Combine fried Italian sausage, cream cheese, ricotta, 1 1/2 cup of mozzarella, parmesan, marinara sauce, Italian seasoning, garlic powder, salt and pepper. Mix until combined.
3. Transfer mixture to a pie dish or skillet. Spread uniformly on remaining mozzarella before sprinkling.
4. Place in the oven and bake for 20 minutes, then broil for 2-3 minutes or until browning starts.
5. Serve with sliced baguette immediately.

8. CHICKEN KABABS

Prep Time: 10 mins

Cook Time: 15 mins

Ingredients

- 2 pounds of dark meat ground chicken
- 3 finely chopped serrano chiles
- 1/3 Cup of chopped cilantro
- 5 tsp ground coriander
- 3 1/2 tsp cumin powder
- 2 tsp garam masala powder
- 1 tsp red chili flakes
- 2 1/2 tsp kosher salt
- 1 Cup of store-bought bread crumbs
- 1 tsp ginger and garlic paste
- 1 lemon juiced
- 1 large grated onion

Instructions

1. Mix all the ingredients.
2. Preheat oven to broil.
3. Place kababs on a silicone baking mat or parchment paper, broil on one side for 8 minutes, turn over and on the other side for 5 minutes.
4. Test kababs' internal temperature to 160 degrees.
5. Sprinkle extra lemon juice.

9. TANDOORI CHICKEN KEBABS

Total Time: 50 mins

Servings: 04

Ingredients

- 1 Cup of low-fat plain yogurt
- Zest of 1 lemon
- 1 tbsp lemon juice
- 1 ½ tbsp tandoori spice blend
- 2 minced cloves garlic
- 2 tbsp divided extra-virgin olive oil
- ¾ tsp divided salt
- ½ tsp divided ground pepper
- 1 pound boneless skinless chicken thighs, trimmed
- 1 large bell pepper
- 1 medium red onion

Instructions

1. In a medium bowl, add yogurt, lemon zest and juice, tandoori seasoning, garlic, 1 tbsp. oil, 1/4 tsp. pepper & 1/2 tsp. salt. Transfer 1/2 cup mixture to a small bowl and cool until ready to use.
2. Mix chicken with the leftover yogurt. Marinate for 20 minutes or refrigerate for 1 day.
3. Grill preheat to big.
4. Add the rest 1 tbsp of oil and 1/4 tsp of salt and pepper in a wide cup. Thread chicken, pepper and onion marinated bits alternately on eight 10- to 12-inch skewers.
5. Reduce medium grill fire. Grill rack gasoline. Check the chicken after six to eight minutes to make sure it is cooked. Serve with the stored yogurt sauce.

Cook's Note

- Make-Ahead Tip: Marinate chicken in the refrigerator for up to 1 day: refrigerate yogurt sauce separately.
- Equipment: Eight 8 to 10-inch skewers.
- An oiled grill rack prevents food from sticking. Grill the chicken and vegetables until they are cooked through, around 6 to 8 minutes per hand.

10. BAKED APPLE CHIPS

Prep Time: 15 mins

Cook Time: 02 Hrs

Servings: 30 Chips

Ingredients

- 2 apples, your favorite variety
- 2 tbsp powdered sugar
- 2 tsp cinnamon

Instructions

1. Heat the oven to 200°F.
2. Line two large parchment or silicone baking pad baking sheets.
3. Sift powdered bowl sugar. Add cinnamon to powdered sugar and mix softly.
4. Thinly slice apples with a mandolin to 1/16-inch. Drop seeds from single slices.
5. Spread apple slices on lined baking sheets, making one layer. Around 15 slices should fit on a half-pan.
6. Shift cinnamon and sugar to a sifter or strainer. Sprinkle each apple slice with a thin cinnamon-sugar mixture.
7. Turn over apple slices and sprinkle with leftover cinnamon-sugar.
8. Bake for 1 Hr and bake for an extra 1 Hr.
9. Take the apples from the oven and allow to rest at room temperature for 5 minutes. If apples aren't crunchy, finish baking in intervals of 15 minutes.
10. Remove apples from the baking sheets and allow to cool thoroughly in an airtight container.

Cook's Note

I. Apple variations may be used. Granny Smith, Fuji, Honeycrisp, or Red Delicious.
II. Work rapidly as apples start browning if left exposed to sunlight for too long.
III. Use 4 apples if you like more slices of the middle star pattern. Slicing from the apple's bottom is finished.
IV. Apple chips can be made without powdered sugar, cinnamon is optional. Using the same recycle instructions.

11. COD NUGGETS

Prep Time: 20 mins

Cook Time: 15 mins

Servings: 04

Ingredients

- 1l vegetable oil for deep-frying
- 300g skinless cod fillet
- 100g plain flour
- Salt & pepper
- 2 beaten medium eggs
- 120g natural breadcrumbs
- 50g rolled oats

Instructions

1. Oats should be dried before crumbly. Add breadcrumbs and set aside.
2. Heat the oil to 170°C.
3. Season the flour, dunk the chunks in the plain flour and shake off any excess. Dip the egg, then roll the breadcrumb and oat mixture.
4. Deep-fry 3-4 minutes in lots before golden brown. Strain on paper and serve in non-paper cones.

12. TEMPURA FISH NUGGETS

Prep Time: 30 mins

Cook Time: 10 mins

Servings: 08

Ingredients

- ¾ cup of plus one tbsp all-purpose flour
- ¼ cup of cornflour
- 1 tbsp corn starch
- ½ tsp kosher salt
- 1 ½ cups of seltzer water
- 2 pounds any flaky white fish
- Canola oil for frying
- Table salt to sprinkle on cooked fish

Instructions

1. The trick is to have very cold batter and very hot oil. The subsequent fried product would have ideal light coating. Temperature batter and oil are keys to performance.
2. Take a small stainless steel bowl and add flours, corn starch, salt and whisk. Place the bowl in the freezer for 20 minutes.
3. Cook oil to 375 F and keep the temp at that level.
4. When the oil is heated and the small bowel is cooled, placed the small bowl into the larger bowl to keep it very cold. It will be tiny.
5. Let it rest five minutes over the ice, whisk again.
6. Dry the fish parts with paper towels, then fry in the batter and drop into the hot oil.
7. They will fall to the bottom and will lift to the surface and float, around 2-3 mins depending on how thick the bits are. You can need to dislodge them with tongs, a spider or strainer right after dropping them in.
8. When fried, remove the spider to a plate lined with paper towels and sprinkle on a little salt. Excavate all the fried batter pieces that float up before cooking the next batch.
9. Serve in tartar sauce baskets or make tacos.

Cook's Note

Realizing so many people don't have access to fresh seafood, I made this with frozen cod loins in my local supermarket's freezer case. Haddock, catfish, sole, or tilapia are other healthy options.

13. CHEESY CHICKEN ENCHILADA DIP

Prep Time: 05 mins

Cook Time: 25 mins

Serves: 10

Ingredients

- 1 packet dry Hidden Valley
- 1 10 oz can red enchilada sauce
- 3 cups of cooked shredded chicken
- 1 4.5 oz can drained diced green chiles
- 1 cup of cheddar cheese
- 2 cups of divided Monterey Jack cheese

Instructions

1. Heat the oven to 350°C. Mix the enchilada sauce and the ranch dressing package in a wide bowl. Stir until there are no clumps left.
2. Then, combine 1 cup of cheddar cheese and 1 cup of Monterey Jack cheese with shredded chicken and green chiles. Mix closely until well blended.
3. In a 13 X 9 baking bowl, add the mixture uniformly. Place the remaining cup of Monterey Jack cheese on top. Bake for 20-25 minutes until the cheese around the edges is melted and bubbly.
4. Using your tortilla chips to serve with.

Nutrition Facts:

Calories: 267kcal Carbohydrates: 4g, Protein: 18g Fat: 13g Cholesterol: 64mg Sodium: 767mg Potassium: 127mg Sugar: 2g Calcium: 255mg Iron: 0.6mg

14. COWBOY CAVIAR RECIPE

Prep & Cook Time: 10 mins + 01 hr

Serves: 12

Ingredients

- 1 can of black beans drained & rinsed
- 1 can corn drained and rinsed
- 3 diced Roma tomatoes & 2 diced avocados
- 1/4 cup of diced red onion
- 1/4 cup of chopped finely cilantro
- Juice of 1 lime & 1/2 tsp salt
- 1/2 cup of Italian dressing

Instructions

1. In a mixing bowl, and add the rice, maize, tomatoes, avocado, onion, and cilantro.
2. Squeeze the avocados with lime juice so they do not brown too easily.
3. Pour in the Italian seasoning and dust with salt. Stir once mixed properly.
4. Cover and chill for one hour in the refrigerator to marinate the flavors together. It's better eaten on the same day. The avocado can begin to brown the next day, but it still tastes amazing!

Nutrition Facts

Calories: 120kcal Carbohydrates: 11g Protein: 2g Fat: 7g Sodium: 326mg Potassium: 312mg Fiber: 4g Sugar: 1g Calcium: 15mgIron: 0.8mg.

15. BACON, SCALLION AND CARAMELIZED ONION DIP

Yield: about 02 Cups

Prep Time: 01 Hr

Ingredients

- 1 cup of cooled caramelized onions
- 6 slices bacon, (¼-inch pieces, cooked crisp)
- 3 scallions, green and white parts, minced
- 1 tsp cider vinegar
- ⅛ tsp cayenne pepper
- 1 ¾ cups of sour cream or Greek yogurt
- Kosher salt and freshly ground black pepper

Instructions

1. In a bowl, stir all of the ingredients together. Use salt and pepper to season as needed.
2. Chill before serving for at least 20 mins (or up to 3 days).

Cook's Note

You can make your caramelized onions up to 2 days in advance and keep them in the fridge until you're ready to use them.

16. EASY CREAMY PROSCIUTTO CRACKER APPETIZER

Prep Time: 10 mins

Cook Time: 01 min

Serves: 40

Ingredients

- 7 oz whipped cream cheese
- 1 tbsp minced garlic
- 1 1/2 tsp olive oil
- 3 ounces sliced Prosciutto
- 40 crackers I used ritz
- Salt and pepper as need
- finely chopped parsley for topping
- Honey for drizzling

Instructions

1. Mix the cream cheese, garlic, olive oil, salt, and pepper in a small bowl. Only cast aside.
2. Cut into tiny rectangles of prosciutto.
3. Using each cracker to disperse a small volume of the mixture until each cracker is thinly coated.
4. Roll up each prosciutto and place the crackers on top.
5. Drizzle with a tiny amount of honey each and sprinkle with partly cold.

Nutrition Facts:

Calories: 42kcal Carbohydrates: 2g Fat: 3g Saturated Fat: 1g Cholesterol: 6mg Sodium: 56mg Potassium: 14mg Calcium: 10mg Iron: 0.2mg

17. CHEESY SAUSAGE DIP

Prep Time: 10 mins

Cook Time: 15 mins

Serves: 24

Ingredients

- 1 lb bulk sausage
- 1 tbsp Worcestershire sauce
- 1 tsp onion powder
- 1/4 tsp garlic powder
- 8 oz sour cream
- 8 oz cream cheese
- 8 oz shredded cheddar cheese
- 4 oz shredded muenster cheese
- 14.5 ounce can Rotel

Instructions

1. Cook the sausage until browned on medium-high heat, breaking off the meat as you cook. And in Worcestershire sauce, onion, and garlic powder, as the meat starts to brown. Drain off the fat until the meat has been fried.
2. Send the pan to the burner again. Turn down the heat to mild.To the mixture, add sour cream, cream cheese, cheddar, muenster, and Rotel, and whisk regularly until the cream cheese is fully melted & mixed properly.
3. Serve with the dippers you prefer. Frito Scoops, Chips of Tortilla, or celery!

Nutrition Facts

Calories: 159kcal Carbohydrates: 1gProtein: 7g Fat: 14g Cholesterol: 41mg Sodium: 253mg Potassium: 92mg Calcium: 127mg Iron: 0.4mg.

18. ANTIPASTI BITES

Prep Time:10 mins

Cook Time: 07 mins

Serves: 08

Ingredients

- 24 slices of Genoa salami 4-inch circles
- 1 cup of marinated artichoke hearts drained & finely chopped
- 1/3 cup of finely chopped jarred roasted red peppers
- 1/4 cup of chopped fresh basil + more for garnishing
- 4 oz fresh mini mozzarella balls

Instructions

1. Place a rack in the middle of the oven and heat it to 400 degrees.
2. Place each muffin cup with one slice of salami. In the cups, press the slices of the salami.
3. Bake until the salami or around 7-10 minutes, is crisp. Leave it out of the oven and leave to cool.
4. Then, in a large bowl, combine the artichoke hearts, roasted peppers, basil, and mozzarella balls.

Cook's Note

You should pre-cook the artichoke mixture and cool it in the refrigerator up to a day in advance.

Place the salami cups on a pan. With an artichoke, coat the mixture. Covering with more minced basil.

19. HONEY GARLIC CROCKPOT MEATBALLS

Prep & Cook Time: 05 mins + 04 hours

Serves: 08

Ingredients

- 1/4 cup of brown sugar
- 1/3 cup of honey
- 1/2 cup of ketchup
- 2 tbsp soy sauce
- 3 minced cloves garlic
- 1 28oz bag fully cooked (frozen meatballs)

Instructions

1. Combine the brown sugar, ketchup, soy sauce, and garlic
2. in a medium bowl of honey.
3. In a 3-4 quart crockpot, place the frozen meatballs and pour the sauce over the meatballs. Stir such that all the meatballs are uniformly covered. Cook for 4 hours at a low temperature, stirring
4. regularly.
5. Using it as an appetizer or deliver a dinner over rice!

Nutrition Facts

Calories: 90kcal Carbohydrates: 22g Sodium: 390mg Potassium: 77mg Sugar: 21g Calcium: 10mg Iron: 0.3mg

20. STUFFED BAGUETTE

Prep Time: 20 mins

Chilling Time: 01 hours 01 min

Serves: 14

Ingredients

- 1 baguette about 14 inches long
- 8 oz cream cheese brought
- 4 oz goat cheese
- 1/4 cup of each of green olives & black olives
- 2 cloves minced garlic
- 2 tbsp of chopped fire-roasted peppers
- 1 tsp dried parsley
- 1.5 oz salami

Instructions

1. Slice the baguette off both ends of it. Next, cut the baguette in half, and make 2, 6 baguettes. This would make hollowing out and things smoother.
2. Use a long thin knife to hollow the baguette and operate on both sides.
3. Leave about half an inch of dense crust all over.
4. The majority of the ingredients are added to the mixing bowl.
5. Mix until well mixed, using an electric mixer/stand mixer.
6. Function on both ends again and cover the baguette with the cheese mixture. Pack the stuffing close.
7. Cover the stuffed baguette in plastic very well and refrigerate for a minimum of two hours and up to two days.
8. Just before eating, cut the baguette into 1/2-inch thick slices and eat.

Cook's Note

Know, if you are not a fan of any of the filling Ingredients above, swap them with things you prefer.

Nutrition Facts

Calories: 119kcal Carbohydrates: 11g Protein: 5g Fat: 6g Cholesterol: 15mg Sodium: 351mg Potassium: 74mg Fiber: 1g Sugar: 1g Calcium: 52mg Iron: 0.8mg

21. GARLIC PARMESAN STICKS

Prep Time: 03 mins

Cook Time: 05 mins

Yield: 04 Servings

Ingredients

- Italian Herb Flat Out
- ⅓ cup of softened cream cheese
- 2 TB minced garlic
- ⅓ cup of shredded Parmesan cheese
- Italian seasoning
- Black pepper

Instructions

1. Cut out part of the Flat Out.
2. Over the Flat Out, spread the softened cream cheese.
3. Over the cream cheese, spread the garlic.
4. Sprinkle on top of shredded Parmesan cheese.
5. Add the black pepper and the Italian seasoning with a sprinkle.
6. Bake at 350*F in an air fryer (or oven) for 5 mins.
7. Cut into sticks.
8. Serve with warm sauce for pizza.

22. PIZZA STICKS

Prep Time: 01 min

Cook Time: 05 mins

Yield: 04 Servings

Ingredients

- Italian Herb Flat Out
- 1/3 cup of softened cream cheese
- 1/3 cup of pizza sauce
- 1/3 cup of shredded mozzarella cheese
- Desired toppings- sliced pepperoni, red pepper flakes, Italian seasoning

Instructions

1. Cut out part of the Flat Out.
2. Onto the Flat Out, spread a layer of softened cream cheese.
3. Add a pizza sauce cover.
4. Add a layer of mozzarella cheese that has been shredded.
5. Add toppings that are wanted.
6. Bake at 350*F for 5 mins in an air fryer.
7. Serve with warm sauce for pizza.

23. HEALTHY BAKED CARROT CHIPS

Prep Time: 20 mins

Cook Time: 20 mins

Total Time: 40 mins

Ingredients

- 2 pounds carrots
- 1/4 cup of olive oil
- 1 tbsp sea salt
- 1 tsp ground cumin
- 1 tsp ground cinnamon

Instructions

1. Heat the oven to 425 F. Set aside and cover some large baking sheets with parchment paper.
2. Trim off the tops of the carrots. The carrots paper-thin on the bias to yield elongated slices beginning on the thick end slice. You may do this with a chef's knife, but it is better to use a mandolin slicer for the smallest setting. Stop and preserve them to be used in soup or salad as you get down to the thin end.
3. In a large bowl, place the carrot slices and add oil, salt, cumin, and cinnamon. Toss well to coat thoroughly.Then lay the slices in one continuous layer on the baking sheets.
4. Bake until the sides start to curl up and turn crisp, for 12-15 mins. Then turn over all the chips and roast to crisp the bottoms for another 5-8 minutes. Store in an airtight jar for 2 weeks, until cooled.

Cook's Note

You should bake the chips for approximately 30 mins at 325 degrees F to prevent tossing the chips. When baked at high temperatures, though, they are prettier.

The chips in the very middle of each pan can take a few minutes longer than the chips around the edges if your oven is older.

Nutrition Facts

Calories: 107kcal, protein: 1g, fat: 7g, carbohydrates: 11g, cholesterol: 0mg, sodium: 950mg, potassium: 367mg, fiber: 3g, sugar: 5g, calcium: 42mg, iron: 0.5mg

1. BBQ BEEF ROAST WITH CORN & PEPPER COUSCOUS

Prep Time: 25 mins

Cook Time: 05 to 5 1/2 Hrs (High)

Servings: 08

Ingredients

- 2-pound boneless beef chuck pot roast
- 1 tsp chili powder
- 1 tsp ground cumin
- ½ tsp garlic salt
- ½ tsp ground black pepper
- 1 ounce can diced tomatoes with garlic & onion
- ¼ Cup of packed brown sugar
- 2 tbsp vinegar
- 2 tbsp Worcestershire sauce
- 1 tbsp quick-cooking crushed tapioca
- ½ tsp dry mustard
- 1 recipe Corn and Pepper Couscous

Instructions

1. Trim meat fat. Stir in a small bowl chili powder, cumin, salt and pepper. Sprinkle mixture uniformly over meat: blend with your fingers. Cut meat, if necessary, in a 3 1/2- or 4-quarter slow cooker. Placed meat in oven.
2. Combine tomatoes, palm sugar, vinegar, Worcestershire sauce, tapioca, and mustard. Pour over fried beef.
3. Cover and simmer for 10-11 Hrs on low-heat or 5-1/2 Hrs on high-heat.
4. Transfer roast to cutting board, reserving liquid cooking. Cut meat in bits.
5. Serve corn and pepper couscous. Drizzle liquid over meat, transfer the remainder. If required, use lime wedges.

Nutrition Facts

371 calories: total fat 14g: cholesterol 56mg: sodium 520mg: potassium 370mg: carbohydrates 38g: fiber 4g: sugar 10g: protein 23g: niacin equivalents 4mg: folate 16mcg: calcium 50mg: iron 4mg.

2. TENDER BBQ BEEF ROAST

Prep Time: 05 mins

Cook Time: 07 Hrs 30 mins

Servings: 04 People

Ingredients

- 2 lb Tri-Tip Roast
- 1/2 Cup of chopped Red Onion
- 3 minced garlic cloves
- 3/4 Cup of Ketchup
- 1/4 Cup of Brown Sugar
- 1 tbsp Chili Powder
- 1 tbsp Yellow Mustard
- 1/4 Cup of Apple Cider Vinegar
- 1 1/2 tsp Paprika
- 1 tbsp Worcestershire Sauce
- 1/4 Cup of Beef Broth

Instructions

1. Next, make the bbq sauce: add all ingredients in a small bowl except the beef roast and blend until well mixed.
2. Pour a third of the crockpot's sauce down. Place beef roast on top of sauce, then pour over remaining sauce.
3. Place cover on crockpot and cook 7 1/2 Hrs on low heat or 4 Hrs on high heat. When finished, beef would be tender fork.
4. Serve with fluffy mashed potatoes, salads or vegetables. You should also serve on toasty sandwich buns! Enjoy it!

Cook's Note

Place residues in an airtight container in the fridge for up to 2-3 days.

Try tip, chuck roast, or London broil. I used a trip tip roast and it was totally delicious!

3. BEEF SHORT RIBS

Prep & Cook Time: 20 mins + 03 Hrs 30 mins

Servings: 06 People

Ingredients

- 5 pounds short ribs about 6 English style ribs
- 1 tsp kosher salt
- 1 tsp ground black pepper
- 3 tbsp vegetable oil
- 1 diced Vidalia onion & 2 diced celery stalks
- 2 minced shallots
- 12 diced baby carrots or 3 medium carrots
- 3 tbsp all-purpose flour
- 1 tbsp tomato paste & 2 tsp kosher salt
- 2 tbsp minced garlic or garlic paste
- 1 tsp ground mustard powder
- ¼ tsp crushed red pepper flakes
- 750 ml Cabernet Sauvignon
- 4 cup of beef stock
- 6 sprigs fresh thyme
- 4 sprigs fresh rosemary & 4 sprigs fresh oregano
- 2 bay leaves fresh

Instructions

1. Season the beef with salt and pepper.
2. Heat the oil over medium-heat in a big Dutch oven, sear the ribs in batches, 2-3 ribs at a time, checking each side for about 45 seconds. Transfer to a plate and finish searing the beef.
3. Remove some of the Dutch oven's extra oil/fat, making sure to leave some. Add celery, onions, shallots and carrots until smooth and transparent, around 5 minutes.
4. Add rice, salt, tomato paste, garlic, mustard powder, and red pepper flakes and mix for about 1 minute.
5. Using the spoon to scrape and deglaze the bottom of the bowl. Add the ribs and spoon the wine over them, allow them to boil and reduce the wine for about 20 minutes. Meanwhile, preheat to 350°F.
6. Add beef stock and herbs and cover for about 2 Hrs and 45 minutes. When its done, meat should fall off the bone.
7. When fried, cut ribs. Skim the extra fat from the top of the sauce and cut the bay leaves.

Nutrition Facts

Calories: 726, Carbohydrates: 19g, Protein: 58g, Fat: 36g, Cholesterol: 163mg, Sodium: 1714mg, Potassium: 1527mg, Fiber: 3g, Sugar: 6g, Calcium: 95mg, Iron: 8mg.

4. KOREAN BARBECUE BEEF SKEWERS

Prep Time: 02 Hrs 45 mins

Cook Time: 10 mins

Servings: 04 People

Ingredients

- 20 ounces flank steak
- ¼ Cup of orange juice fresh
- ¼ Cup of soy sauce low sodium
- 3 cloves garlic minced
- 2 tbs ginger grated
- 2 tbs fish sauce
- 2 tbs rice wine vinegar
- ½ tbs chili garlic paste
- ¼ Cup of scallions chopped

Instructions

1. In long, thin strips, slice flank steak against the grain and place in a large glass dish or plastic bag.
2. Pour over the remaining ingredients and marinate for 2 Hrs or longer. Place wooden skewers in a shallow dish and cover with water. This avoids skewers burning while grilling.
3. It's safer to cook the beef 20 minutes until it is at room temperature.
4. Heat the grill pan and add non-stick spray.
5. Skewer beef and barbecue for 2-3 minutes.
6. Serve with onions and cucumbers.

Cook's Note

The sodium number is based on the maximum volume of marinade, but please remember that 75% of the marinade persists after removal.

Nutrition Facts

Calories: 203kcal, Carbohydrates: 5.3g, Protein: 27.8g, Fat: 6.9g, Cholesterol: 40mg, Sodium: 1522mg, Fiber: 0.2g.

5. KOREAN BRAISED BEEF SHORT RIBS

Prep Time: 15 mins

Cook Time: 06 Hrs

Ingredients

- 1 thinly sliced vertically medium onion
- 8 sliced large cloves garlic
- 2 cup of beef broth
- 1/2 Cup of soy sauce, coconut aminos or tamari
- 1/4 Cup of coconut sugar or brown sugar
- 2 tbsp unseasoned rice vinegar
- 1 tbsp dark sesame oil & 2 tbsp gochujang
- 2 tbsp + 1 tsp canola, vegetable or peanut oil
- Salt and black pepper
- 4 long-cut bone-in beef short ribs, trimmed of excess fat
- 2 tbsp cornstarch & 2 tbsp minced ginger
- 2 trimmed bunches scallions
- 2 tbsp toasted sesame seeds
- Shredded carrots & Kimchi
- Cooked brown rice

Instructions

1. Combine the first 9 ingredients in a cooker. Set slow cooker to preheat.
2. Heat 2 tbsp of oil in a large skillet over medium-high heat.
3. Season generously with salt and black pepper. Add short ribs, minimize heat to low, and brown well on all sides, between 2-3 minutes per side.
4. Transfer ribs, beef side-down, slow cooking.
5. Cover for 4-6 Hrs or before really tender.
6. Combine cornstarch in a small bowl with around 4 tbsp cooking liquid and stir until smooth. Pour the cornstarch mixture into a slow cooker, blend and simmer uncovered for about 20 minutes.
7. Turn off and let stand 10 minutes.
8. Heat the remaining 1 tsp. oil in a skillet over medium-high. Cook scallions, 2-3 minutes or until slightly browned.
9. Serve with scallions, kimchi, brown rice, and shredded carrots.

Cook's Note

MAKE AHEAD: Reheat beef short ribs wonderfully. Reheat 30-40 minutes in a 350-degree oven or until heated.

FREEZER-FRIENDLY: Cool fully, pack in an airtight container and freeze up to 3 months. Thaw in the refrigerator and run for 30-40 minutes.

6. BEEF NOODLE CASSEROLE

Prep Time: 10 mins

Cook Time: 30 mins

Total Time: 40 mins

Ingredients

- 12 ounces egg noodles
- 2 tsp olive oil
- 1 1/4 lbs lean ground beef
- 1 finely chopped onion
- 2 tsp minced garlic
- salt and pepper as need
- 16 ounces canned tomato sauce
- 15 ounce can diced tomatoes drained
- 2 tsp Italian seasoning
- 2 Cup of shredded cheddar cheese
- 2 tbsp chopped parsley

Instructions

1. Bring a bowl of salted water: add egg noodles and cook according to the instructions of the box. Preheat the oven to 400°F.
2. When frying, heat the olive oil in a wide pan over medium heat.
3. Add the ground beef and cook 4-5 minutes, cutting the meat with a spatula.
4. Add the onion, garlic, simmer for another 5 minutes or until the onion has softened and the beef is cooked through. Salt and pepper as appropriate.
5. Add tomato sauce, onions, and Italian beef seasoning and stir to blend.
6. Drain the noodles and add the beef to the saucepan.
7. In a 9'x13' baking pan covered with cooking oil, pour the beef and noodle mixture into a. Cheddar cheese top.
8. Bake 10-15 minutes or until melted. Sprinkle with parsley.

7. BAKED BBQ BEEF RIBS

Prep & Cook Time: 10 mins + 04 Hrs

Marinate Time: 02 Hrs

Servings: 04 People

Ingredients

- 3 lbs meaty beef ribs
- 2-4 tbsp olive oil
- 1 tbsp garlic powder
- 1 tbsp onion powder
- 1 tbsp cajun seasoning
- 2 tbsp dark brown sugar packed
- 1 tsp chili powder
- 1 tsp salt can use smoked salt as well.
- 1 tsp paprika
- 2 tsp oregano

Instructions

1. Rinse ribs, rinse with paper towels.
2. Douse dried ribs with liquid smoke and rub them in.
3. Cover ribs in olive oil.
4. Season and scatter gently over ribs, front and back.
5. Massage spices into the ribs, adding more olive oil to spread spices further if necessary.
6. Place ribs in a big ziplock bag or covered bowl and marinate 1-2 Hrs in the fridge.
7. Heat the oven to 250 F.
8. Place ribs in one layer on a foil-lined baking tray.
9. Add another layer of foil on top for the ribs to cook in. Seal the corners of the foil so it's close and steam won't seep out.
10. Bake 3 1/2-4 Hrs on mid-rack. Review after 3 1/2 hrs mark. The oven temperature is low, so you can cook it a little longer without concern.
11. When done to your taste, drain the extra fat.
12. Brush ribs with desired BBQ sauce.
13. Broil low before sauce moist.
14. Serve hot, enjoy!

8. GRILLED BEEF KABOBS

Prep Time: 15 mins

Cook Time: 10 mins

Servings: 08

Ingredients

- 2.5 lbs beef tenderloin cubed
- 3 whole bell cubed peppers
- 1 medium onion cubed
- Reynolds Wrap Heavy Duty Foil
- Skewers

Beef Marinade:

- 2 tbsp lightly flavored olive oil
- 2 tbsps minced fresh garlic
- 2 tbsps soy sauce
- 2 tbsp Worcestershire sauce
- 1 tbsp balsamic vinegar
- 1 tbsp black pepper fresh cracked

Instructions

1. Cube the steak, peppers and onions if you want.
2. Marinate beef cubes with ingredients marinade. Cover and sit in fridge for 30 minutes.
3. When the beef marinates, beef cubes and veggies assemble the skewers.
4. Remove a long foil pan, about 16-18 inches long, and lay it flat on the counter or tray. Place skewers onto the foil sheet core.
5. Bring the foil's long edges, so the ends touch over the food. Doubt fold the ends, allowing heat to flow inside. Seal all short ends. The skewers end up not closing completely, don't think too much. See blog videos.
6. To stop puddling juices around the food, use a skewer to put holes on the packet's rim.
7. Grill the skewers for about 5 minutes, then change the skewers over to grill another 5 minutes. Grilling time varies on your liking.
8. Place the skewers in aluminium foil.
9. Garnish with some parsley and eat with BBQ and side salad.

Cook's Note

Marinate the beef for 30 minutes and 24 Hrs.

For these kebobs, you can use metal skewers or wooden ones, but make sure to soak them in water first.

Heat the barbecue to cook the beef evenly by using a gas grill.

Grilling time can vary with several factors such as type of grill, distance from flames, cooking preferences, etc. Grill accordingly.

To stop puddling juices around the meal, use a skewer to place holes at the bottom of the package.

Nutrition Facts

Calories: 435kcal | Carbohydrates: 3g| Fat: 34g | Cholesterol: 99mg | Sodium: 392mg | Potassium: 484mg | Fiber: 1g | Sugar: 1g | Calcium: 16mg | Iron: 4mg | Protein: 26g .

9. BEEF KEBABS RECIPE

Prep Time: 45 mins

Cook Time: 15 mins

Yield: Serves 4 to 6

Ingredients

- 1/3 Cup of ex. virgin olive oil
- 1/3 Cup of soy sauce
- 3 tbsp red wine vinegar
- 1/4 Cup of honey
- 2 minced cloves garlic
- 1 tbsp minced fresh ginger
- Freshly ground black pepper as need

Kebab Ingredients:

- 1 1/2 pounds top sirloin steak
- 1 large bell pepper
- 1 - 2 medium red onions
- 1/2 - 1 pound button mushrooms

Instructions

1. In a bowl, mix the marinade ingredients and add the beef. Cover and relax for at least 30 minutes, ideally several Hrs or even overnight.
2. Let the skewers soak for 30 minutes. It would ideally discourage the charcoal from burning.
3. Thread the meat and veggies through the skewers: cut the vegetables into chunks around the beef pieces diameter. Cover meat and vegetables in bamboo skewers.
4. To cut a board securely, set up a board on top of the object and push skewers into both the board and the object.
5. Double skewers help transform the kebabs on the grill. If you leave any distance between the bits, they'll grill equally.
6. Paint kebabs with the leftover marinade.
7. Grill on high, direct heat: ready your grill for strong, direct heat. Grill for 8-10 minutes depending on how hot your grill is and how good you like your meat turning sometimes.
8. Let the meat rest 5 mins than serving.

10. SPICY MEXICAN BEEF BAKE

Total Time: 01 Hr 30 mins

Servings: 08

Ingredients

- 1-1/2 pounds Ground Beef
- 3 cans divided mild enchilada sauce
- 1 tbsp packed brown sugar
- 1 can black beans, rinsed, drained
- 3/4 Cup of chopped red bell pepper
- 1/3 Cup of diced celery
- 1/3 Cup of diced onion
- 1-1/2 tsp ground cumin
- 15 corn tortillas
- 1 Cup of shredded reduced-fat Mexican cheese blend

Instructions

1. Heat the oven to 400°F. Combine enchilada sauce and brown bowl syrup, stirring until sugar is dissolved. Set aside.
2. Heat broad skillet over medium heat until hot. Add ground beef: cook 8-10 minutes, crumble 1/2-inch, and stir periodically. Garnish drippings if necessary.
3. Bring 2-1/2 cup sauce combination, rice, bell pepper, celery, onion and cumin to a boil. Reduce heat: cook 5 minutes, stirring periodically.
4. Spray 13 x 9-inch glass baking spray dish. Spread half of the remaining sauce mixture over the baking dish. Arrange 5 tortillas over sauce, slightly overlapping: top with 1/2 beef mixture and 1/4 cup cheese. Repeat once for all left beef mixture, 5 tortillas and 1/4 cup cheese. Cover with 5 left tortillas and sauce mixture, spreading uniformly to moist tortillas. Reserve 1/2 cup of cheese.
5. Cover with tape. Bake 30 to 35 minutes in 400°F oven or until heated, bubbly. Sprinkle of preserved cheese. Bake 2 or 3 mins, until cheese is melted. Let stand 10 minutes, uncovered. Cut 8 servings. Using sour cream, if needed.

Cook's Note

Cooking times are raw or thawed ground beef. Heat ground beef at 160°F internal temperature. Color is not an accurate beef doneness predictor.

Nutrition Facts

349 Calories, Total Fat 67mg, Cholesterol: 696mg, Sodium: 38g, Total Carbohydrate: 6.2g, Dietary Fiber: 27g, Protein: 3.7mg, Iron: 5.5mg, Zinc: 16.5 mcg.

11. BEEF KABOBS WITH CORN AND ORZO SALAD

Total Time: 25 mins

Servings: 06

Ingredients

- 4 tsp chili powder
- 2 tsp garlic salt
- 1 tsp ground cumin
- 1 tsp oregano
- 1 ½ pounds boneless beef sirloin steak
- ⅔ Cup of dried orzo pasta
- 2 Cup of fresh corn kernels
- 1 chopped medium bell pepper
- ½ Cup of thinly sliced red onion
- ⅔ Cup of halved grape tomatoes
- 1 tsp lime zest
- ¼ Cup of lime juice
- 2 tbsp chopped fresh cilantro
- 2 tbsp olive oil
- Lime wedges

Instructions

1. In a resealable plastic container, combine chili powder, cumin, and oregano. Add bits of beef, a handful at a time. Thread meat on skewers, 1/4 inch between each piece.
2. Grill meat skewers, wrapped, 8 to 12 minutes over medium heat or until meat is slightly pink in the middle, rotating skewers once or twice during grilling.
3. Meanwhile, cook orzo according to box instructions, adding last-minute cooking corn. Drain the colander. Rinse: re-drain. Combine orzo, chili, cabbage, and tomatoes in a large bowl.
4. For the dressing: mix lime zest and juice, 2 Tbsp. Olive oil, cilantro, 1/2 tsp. Salt. Salt. Cover, shake good. Pour over orzo mixture: toss to cover. Serve corn and orzo salad on a large tray. Top with meat skewers and cilantro if desired. Serve lime wedges.

Nutrition Facts

305 calories: total fat 11g: cholesterol 61mg: sodium 431mg: potassium 703mg: carbohydrates 31g: fiber 4g: sugar 6g: protein 25g: trans fatty acid 0g: calcium 33mg: iron 4mg.

12. TUSCAN BEEF & PESTO PASTA

Total Time: 30 mins

Make Servings: 04

Ingredients

- 1 package refrigerated fully cooked boneless beef pot roast with gravy
- 8 ounces uncooked whole grain rotini pasta
- 3/4 Cup of sliced ripe olives
- 1 large red bell pepper
- 1 can diced tomatoes with roasted garlic
- 3 tbsp prepared basil pesto sauce
- 1/2 tsp pepper

Instructions

1. Cook pasta as instructed by package: drain and keep warm.
2. Meanwhile cut pot roast from package: pass gravy to broad casserole. Cut roast pot into 1/2-inch pieces: add to saucepan. Reserve 1 tbsp of each olive and pepper strip: set aside.
3. Add tomatoes to casserole: carry to a simmer. Drop pesto and olives: boil for 7 minutes. Add remaining pepper strips and pepper: boil 5 minutes.
4. Combine beef and pasta in a bowl: toss well. Cover with olives and pepper strips.

Nutrition Facts

Calories: 198.9, Total Fat 53mg, Cholesterol: 937mg, Sodium: 56g, Total Carbohydrate: 9.2g, Dietary Fiber: 25g, Protein: 3.5mg, Iron: 500mg, Potassium: 5.3mg, NE Niacin: 0.3mg, Zinc: 43.6mcg.

13. THAI BASIL BEEF

Prep Time: 10 min

Cook Time: 15 min

Serves: 04

Ingredients

- 2 tbsp Olive oil or vegetable oil
- 1 lb Ground beef
- 1 thinly sliced bell pepper
- 1 thinly sliced sweet onion
- 6 minced garlic cloves
- 1 cup of divided loosely packed fresh basil leaves
- Thai Basil Beef Sauce
- 1 tbsp Chili paste
- 2 tbsp Soy sauce
- 1 tbsp Fish sauce
- 1 tbsp Brown sugar
- 2 tbsp fresh lime juice

Instructions

1. Combine the chili paste, soy sauce, fish sauce, brown sugar, and lime juice in a small bowl before ready to set aside.
2. In a large skillet set to over medium heat, heat the oil. Add the ground beef and cook until browned, divided with a spoon, stirring frequently around 6 minutes.
3. Add the bell pepper, onion, and garlic to the beef and simmer for about 5 minutes, before the vegetables begin to soften.
4. Pour the mixture of the sauce along with the fresh basil and continue to cook until the basil begins to wilt.
5. Serve over rice topped with fresh coriander and fresh basil. Enjoy!

Cook's Note

Add 1/2 tsp of salt to ground beef if low-sodium soy sauce is used.

14. GINGERY GROUND BEEF

Recipe Time: 30 mins

Ingredients

- 1 lb Ground beef
- 1/3 cup of Soy sauce
- 1/4 cup of Water
- 1 tbsp Sugar
- 1 tbsp minced fresh ginger
- 1 cup of frozen peas

Instructions

1. Mix the ground beef, soy sauce, water, and sugar in a large skillet and cook over medium heat until the beef is only browned.
2. Add fresh ginger and frozen peas and continue to cook until the liquid is mostly evaporated.
3. Serve over rice that is cooked.

15. CLASSIC CHEESE BURGER WITH SECRET SAUCE

Prep & Cook Time: 15 min + 35 min

Serves: 04

Ingredients

- 2 tbsp Olive oil
- 2 thinly sliced yellow onions
- 2 lbs lean grass-fed ground beef
- 2 Eggs
- 1/2 cup of grated yellow onion
- 3 tsp granules garlic powder
- 2 tbsp Worcestershire
- 2 tsp Mustard powder
- 2 tsp salt + more for seasoning patties
- 1 tsp Freshly ground pepper
- 1 sliced tomato
- 4 slices cheddar cheese
- 4 Romaine lettuce leaves
- 4 Brioche hamburger buns

Secret Sauce:

- 1 cup of Mayonnaise
- 2 tbsp Ketchup
- 1/2 tsp Garlic powder
- 2 tbsp Pickle juice
- 2 tsp Lime juice & 1 tsp Dried dill
- 1 tsp smoked paprika
- 1/2 tsp Cayenne pepper
- 1 tsp ground mustard

Instructions

1. In a small bowl, whisk together the secret sauce components until smooth. Cover when used, then refrigerate. It can be maintained for up to one week in an airtight container.
2. Heat olive oil over low heat in a medium-sized, heavy-bottom saucepan. Add the thinly sliced onion rings and sauté until caramelized, over medium-low heat. 25-35 min roughly. Lower the heat if they start browning too fast. Cast aside until done.
3. Ground beef, eggs, grilled cabbage, garlic, Worcestershire, mustard, sea salt, and pepper in a wide bowl. Use your hands to blend the meat until it's thoroughly mixed. Divide the beef into four equal portions and mold it around 1/3 inch thick into patties. On parchment paper, set aside.
4. Heat the high grill for 10 min.
5. Season with a little salt and pepper on each patty and place on the hot grill. Lower the heat to low, then close the lid. For 5 mins, cook. Flip and cook the burger patties for another 3-5 minutes, just until the middle is barely yellow. To the patties, add the cheese, cover the cover and let it melt free. Using your hot grill to toast your buns while the cheese is melting!
6. Add a pinch of hidden sauce to both the top and bottom of the toasted bun to cook the cheeseburgers. The beef patties are added, then the lettuce, onions, and tomatoes are layered. Using for pickles to serve.

16. MEATBALL SUB SANDWICH

Prep Time: 10 min

Cook Time: 25 min

Total Time: 35 mins

Serves: 06

Ingredients

- 1 lb Ground beef
- 1/2 lb ground mild Italian sausage,
- 4 finely chopped Garlic cloves
- Finely chopped Italian parsley, 1/3 cup
- 1/2 cup of Italian style bread crumbs
- 1 Egg
- 3/4 cup of freshly grated Parmesan cheese
- 1 tsp Salt
- 1 tsp freshly ground Pepper
- 3 cups of Marinara sauce, store-bought
- 6 Hoagie rolls
- 4 tbsp Olive oil
- 2 tsp Garlic powder
- 8 oz shredded Mozzarella cheese
- Etc.

Instructions

1. Place in a wide bowl the steak, bacon, parsley, garlic, bread crumbs, egg, parmesan, salt & pepper. Using your hands to mix the meatball ingredients until they are thoroughly mixed and be careful not to overwork the mixture. Roll into 24 meatballs, around 2 tbsp each, before all Ingredients are mixed.
2. In a large saucepan, add the marinara and meatballs and bring to a low boil. Using a lid to protect and cook for 10 mins. Uncover it and simmer for 10 more minutes.
3. Brush the interior of hoagie rolls with olive oil as the meatballs are frying, then dust with garlic powder.
4. Broiler with Fire. Set up hoagie rolls in a 9X13 baking dish and add 4 meatballs to each roll. Top with mozzarella on each meatball sub. Spot the preparing dish under the grill and cook until the cheddar is dissolved.
5. Place extra parsley on top and enjoy!

17. MEATBALL SHAKSHUKA

Prep Time: 15 min

Cook Time: 50 min

Serves: 06

Ingredients

- 2 tbsp Olive oil
- 2 Bell peppers (red and green)
- 1 thinly sliced Onion
- 2 tsp Cumin
- 2 tsp smoked paprika
- 1/2 tsp Salt
- 1 28 oz can whole stewed tomatoes
- 1 lb Ground beef
- 2 tsp smoked paprika
- 2 tsp Cumin
- 1/2 tsp Salt
- 2 minced Garlic cloves
- 1 finely chopped Bunch of cilantro
- 2 Eggs
- 1 cup of Bread crumbs

Instructions

1. In a skillet with a wide cover, melt 2 teaspoons of olive oil over medium high heat.
2. Add the onions and peppers, stirring often until the onions are nearly caramelized. About 10 minutes. Add the cumin, salt, and smoked paprika and stir until fragrant.
3. Use your hands to smash the tomatoes one at a time and add the remaining liquid from the pan to the pepper and onion mixture. Bring the mixture to a boil and allow it to cook until it starts to thicken. Change the seasoning as needed.
4. Mix the ground beef along with all the meatball Ingredients as the sauce is thickening and swirl using the hands and be vigilant not to over-mix.
5. Use your hands to form meatballs about the size of golf balls.
6. Arrange the meatballs carefully in the sauce to get it up to a boil. Cover the pan and finish cooking for 10 mins on low heat. Uncover it and simmer for 10 more minutes. When the meatballs exceed an internal temperature of 165 ° F on an instant-read thermometer, they are cooked.
7. Good meatballs with fresh cilantro and feta. Serve with pita bread or toasted bread.

18. SWEDISH MEATBALLS

Serves: 08

Ingredients

Meatballs:

- 1 lb ground beef
- 1 lb ground pork
- ¼ cup of minced Flat-leaf parsley
- ½ tsp Ground allspice
- ½ tsp Ground nutmeg
- ¾ cup of grated Yellow onion
- 2 tsp Salt
- ½ tsp freshly ground Pepper
- 4 minced cloves garlic
- ¾ cup of Panko
- 2 Eggs
- 2 tbsp Olive oil

Cream Gravy:

- ½ cup of Butter
- ½ cup of Flour
- 4 cups of Beef broth
- 1 tsp Salt
- ¼ tsp Pepper
- 1 tbsp Lemon juice
- ¼ tsp Ground allspice
- ¼ tsp Ground nutmeg
- 1 cup of Heavy cream

Instructions

1. Mix the beef, pork, parsley, allspice, nutmeg, grated onion, cinnamon, pepper, garlic, panko, and eggs in a big bowl until well mixed.
2. Measure out the meat mixture into about 35 balls using a tbsp or cookie scoop.
3. Warmth 2 tbsp of olive oil over medium-high warmth in a wide container. Add 1/2 of the meatballs and then roast on both sides until browned. It takes about 5 minutes.
4. Pour out the extra fat in the skillet until all the meatballs are browned, into a heatproof vessel. Lower the heat to mild and add the pan with the butter. Sprinkle in the flour as the butter starts to bubble and cook for 1 min. Add the beef broth a little at a time to the pan.

5. Whisk the gravy until it is all mixed into the soup. Add cinnamon, pepper, lemon juice, nutmeg, and allspice. Whisk in a few times. Add the cream steadily.
6. Add the meatballs back into the pan until the gravy starts to boil.
7. Simmer until the gravy has thickened a little and the meatballs are cooked for around 8-10 mins all the way through.
8. Serve warm alongside steamed vegetables and lingonberry jam over mashed potatoes or egg noodles.

19. LASAGNA SOUP

Prep Time: 10 min

Cook Time: 30 min

Total Time: 40 mins

Serves: 08

Ingredients

- 1 lb ground Italian sausage
- ½ lb Lean ground beef
- 1 diced Onion
- 6 minced cloves garlic
- 1 can crushed tomatoes
- 1 can Tomato paste
- 1 can Tomato sauce
- 4 cups of Chicken broth
- 1 tsp Fennel seeds
- 2 tsp Italian seasoning
- 2 tsp Salt
- ½ tsp Black pepper
- 8 cooked lasagna noodles
- 8 oz shredded Mozzarella
- ½ cup of Parmesan cheese

Instructions

1. Warmth 1 tbsp. olive oil over medium-high warmth in an enormous stock tank. Add the ground hamburger, hotdog, and onions and dish for around 8 minutes, until the meat is carmelized. Add the garlic most of the way into cooking the hamburger.

2. Pour in the tomato glue, canned tomatoes, pureed tomatoes, chicken stock, Italian flavoring, salt, pepper, and fennel until the meat is cooked through, and bubble on low for 20 mins.

3. Prepare the lasagna noodles in a different pot according to product instructions when the soup is heating, and drain.

4. To the pot, add the cooked lasagna noodles and stir to mix them. Garnish with the mozzarella and parmesan cheeses, and some fresh parsley. Enjoy.

5. This soup can safely be used for milk or gluten allergies. The soup itself is dairy-free, just top it before consuming it with a non-dairy cheese replacement. Sub noodles without gluten for a delicious wheat-free soup!

20. BEEF EMPANADAS

Prep Time: 30 min

Cook Time: 55 min

Serves: 08

Ingredients

- Crust:
- 2 1/2 cups of Flour
- 1/2 tsp Salt
- 4 oz Butter, chilled
- 1Egg
- 1/3 cup ofIce water
- 1Egg, beaten for egg wash
- 1Large russet potato, peeled
- 3/4 lb ground Beef
- 2 tbsp Olive oil
- ½ grated Medium onion
- 1 grated Small carrot
- 1 finely minced Rib of celery
- 2 minced cloves of garlic
- 1/2 tsp Chili powder
- 1 tsp ground cumin
- 1/2 tsp ground cinnamon
- 1/2 cup of Peas
- 3/4 cup of Beef broth
- 1/2 tsp Salt
- 1/2 tsp Pepper

Instructions

1. Pulse the flour and salt into a food processor to produce the pastry dough. Add the butter, ice water, and egg. Pulse before coarse crumbs resembles the mixture. Shape a ball into the dough. Firmly cover the batter in saran wrap and spot for in any event 30 minutes in the fridge.

2. Then mix the filling while the empanada dough is resting. Flush a 3/4 full medium-size stockpot with water and bring to a boil. To the pot, add the cubed potato and boil the potato until tender, around 3 mins.

3. Earthy colored the hamburger in a saute skillet over medium warmth alongside the onions, celery, and carrots while the potatoes are bubbling. At the point when the potatoes are done, wash and add them to the combination of ground meat and cook until the hamburger is cooked and the vegetables are mellowed.

4. To the beef and vegetable mixture, add the garlic, chili powder, cumin, cinnamon, and beef broth and sauté for 1 min until the spices are fragrant. Add the peas and boil over medium heat until all is well combined and much of the liquid is absorbed. With salt and pepper, season.

5. Take the mixture from the cooler and cut it into 10 equivalent parts of around 2.2 oz each. Roll each piece of batter on a delicately floured surface until you have a circle around 7 creeps across. A heaping 1/3 cup of filling is added to one side of the dough by dealing with one prepared dough at a time.

6. With egg wash, wet a pastry brush and dampen the inner 1/4 inch edge of the filled dough. Fold in half the dough. Press the sides together tightly with a fork. With the remaining dough and filling, repeat this process and put it on a baking sheet lined with parchment.

7. The oven is heated to 375 degrees F and the rack is placed in the center of the oven.

8. Mix the egg and 1 tablespoon of water in a small bowl and spray each empanada with egg wash until it's sealed. Bake for 35 minutes or until brown and golden brown.

21. GROUND BEEF TOSTADAS

Prep Time: 15 mins

Cook Time: 50 mins

Servings: 08

Ingredients

- 1 1/2 lbs ground beef
- 1 tsp salt
- 1 tbsp chili powder
- 1 tsp Mexican preferred oregano
- 1 tsp ground cumin
- 1 diced large white onion
- 2 seeded and diced jalapeños
- 1/4 cup of tomato paste
- 16 oz diced roasted tomatoes
- 2 seeded and diced large carrots
- 1 large Yukon Gold potato diced

Assembly:

- Corn Tostadas
- 2 cups of Refried Beans
- Green Cabbage sliced thin
- Cotija or Queso Fresco cheese
- Mexican Crema
- Pickled Red Onions
- Cilantro chopped

Instructions

1. Add the ground beef, kosher salt, chili powder, oregano, and cumin over medium-high heat in a dutch oven or large stockpot. Cook for 6-7 minutes until it's no longer pink.
2. Stir in the onion, tomato paste, and jalapeños. Several minutes to cook. Combine the tomatoes with their juices. Drop the fire to a low level and simmer for 20 minutes.
3. For a further 20 minutes, add diced potatoes and carrot, stir and finish cooking. If it is too thick and does not scorch the bottom of the kettle, mix occasionally and add more water.
4. On each tostada shell, assemble by spreading some refried beans and top with ground beef mixture. Add chopped cabbage, cheese, cream, chopped cilantro, and pickled red onion.

22. BEEF KOFTA KABABS WITH TZATZIKI

Prep & Cook Time: 20 mins + 10 mins

Serves: 04

Ingredients

- Kofta
- 2 lb Ground beef
- ½ grated Onion
- 2 minced Garlic cloves
- 1 tsp ground pepper
- 1/2 tsp Sea salt
- 1 tsp Rosemary
- 1 tsp Cumin
- 1 tsp Oregano
- 1/2 tsp Cinnamon

Instructions

Grill Method:

1. Heat the grill over low heat.
2. Run the onions with the grating attachment via a food processor, or grate them by hand. On a paper towel, lay the grated onion and press it to wring out any remaining liquid.
3. In a mixing bowl, add the onion, garlic, ground beef, pepper, salt, rosemary, cumin, oregano, sumac, and cinnamon together. Using your hands to blend the meat and spices.
4. Meat can be fried right away, but if it has time to rest, it may taste better. The beef kofta mixture can also be cooked a day in advance and refrigerated before you're ready to serve.
5. Using one hand to mould the meat and the other to carry the skewer to cram about half a cup of meat around the end of each skewer.
6. Place the meat on the oiled, heated grill and cook until cooked through, turning the skewers with tongs every 2-3 minutes for 8-10 minutes in total.

Baked Method:

1. Heat the oven to 350 degrees.
2. Follow the following measures 2-4.
3. Arrange the kofta on a lightly greased or lined baking sheet and bake for 30 minutes, rotating halfway through.

23. TACO PIZZA

Prep Time: 20 mins

Cook Time: 15 mins

Servings: 04

Ingredients

- 1 lb ground beef
- 1 small white onion chopped
- 1 package taco seasoning
- 1 can refried beans
- 2 tsp chili powder
- 1 tsp cumin
- 1 store-bought pizza dough crust rolled out
- Cornmeal or flour for dusting
- 2 cups of mozzarella cheese shredded
- 2 cups of iceberg lettuce shredded
- ½ cup of sour cream
- 1 cup of chopped tomatoes
- 1 2.25 ounces can of sliced black olives
- Thinly sliced Pepperoncini

Instructions

1. Set a pizza stone on the oven's bottom and heat the oven to 450 degrees.
2. Brown the meat & onions in a pan set over medium heat, until fully cooked and tender. Uh, drain. Follow the instructions on the seasoning taco box. Only set aside.
3. Combine the refried beans with chili powder and cumin in a small bowl and blend until thoroughly integrated.
4. Stretch a 12-inch round with the pizza dough and transfer to a cutting board for cornmeal or flour-dusted.
5. On top, scatter the bean mixture, leaving a 1/2-inch border. Sprinkle with 3/4 of the cheese, then the remaining cheese, followed by the taco beef.
6. Slide the pizza on the hot stone and heat until the foundation is fresh and 12-15 minutes of the cheddar bubbles are fresh. Place the spinach, sour cream dollops, onions, olives, and peppers on top.
7. Slice into eight wedges and serve.

1. ROASTED LEG OF LAMB

Prep & Cook Time: 20 mins + 01 Hr 45 mins

Yield: 08 to 10 Servings

Ingredients

- 1 trimmed bone-in leg of lamb
- 4 minced cloves garlic
- 1 tbsp olive oil
- 1 tbsp chopped fresh rosemary
- 1 tbsp chopped fresh thyme leaves
- 1 tbsp dijon mustard
- 1 tbsp kosher salt
- 2 tsp ground black pepper

Instructions

1. Heat the oven to 350F. Strip aluminum foil roasting pan.
2. Pat lamb with paper towels. Using a sharp knife, score the lamb's topside by shallow slices.
3. Combine garlic, olive oil, rosemary, thyme, dijon, salt and pepper.
4. Roast the lamb on the side that has fat. Spread garlic over the lamb uniformly, rubbing thoroughly into the scored slices.
5. Place in the oven & roast until medium to 135 degrees F indoor temperature, around 1 hrs 30 mins - 1 hrs 45 mins or until desired doneness. Rest 15 minutes before chopping.
6. Serve instantly with mini-potatoes.

2. LEMONY GRILLED LAMB KEBABS AND VEGETABLES

Hands-On Time: 15 mins

Total Time: 25 mins

Yield: Serves: 08

Ingredients

- 3 ½ pounds lamb top round or boneless leg
- 3 tbsp olive oil
- 1 tsp dried oregano
- Kosher salt and black pepper
- 4 seeded bell peppers
- 2 medium red onions, each cut into 6 wedges
- ⅓ Cup of fresh lemon juice + lemon wedges for serving

Instructions

1. Soak 16 skewers in water. Heat medium-high barbecue.
2. Thread the skewers calf. Season with 1 tbsp of oil, 1 tsp of salt and 1/2 tsp of pepper.
3. Toss bell peppers & onions in a large bowl with the remaining 2 tbsp oil, 1/2 tsp salt & 1/4 tsp pepper.
4. Grill the lamb and vegetables, turn regularly and brush with lemon juice until medium-rare and soft, 8 to 10 minutes.

Nutrition Facts

726 calories: fat 55g: cholesterol 175mg: sodium 611mg: protein 47g: carbohydrates 11g: sugars 6g: fiber 2g: iron 5mg: calcium 51mg.

3. MIDDLE EASTERN LAMB SKEWERS

Total Time: 30 mins

Yield: 04 Servings

Ingredients

- 1 quartered medium onion
- 1 peeled garlic clove
- 4 flat-leaf parsley sprigs
- 1/2 tsp finely grated lemon zest
- 3 tbsp fresh lemon juice
- 1 tsp ground allspice
- 1 tbsp kosher salt
- Pinch of saffron threads
- 1 1/4 pounds trimmed lamb loin
- 2 tbsp vegetable oil
- Warm pita and Greek-style plain yogurt for serving

Instructions

1. Combine onion, garlic, parsley sprigs, lemon zest, lemon juice, allspice, salt, saffron and puree until smooth. Transfer the marinade to a plastic resealable container, add the cubed lamb, and transform to coat. Seal the bag, press some air. Refrigerate at least 6 Hrs.
2. Flash a barbecue or grill pan. Drain the lamb, brushing off marinade. Thread the lamb on 4 long skewers, leaving space between the cubes.
3. Brush the lamb with oil and grill over high heat, rotating periodically for medium-rare meat around 5 minutes before finely charred. Serve the soft pita skewers with yogurt.

4. BRAISED GREEK LAMB SHANKS

Prep Time: 30 mins

Cook Time: 03 Hrs

Yield: 04 Servings

Ingredients

- 2 lamb shanks
- 1 1/2 pounds each

For the Spice Rub:

- 1 tsp garlic powder
- 2 tsp onion powder
- 1 tsp cumin powder
- 1/2 tsp smoky paprika
- 2 tsp coarse ground salt
- 1/2 tsp pepper
- 2 tbsp olive oil
- 1 chopped large onion
- 6 thinly sliced cloves garlic
- 3/4 Cup of freshly squeezed lemon juice
- 2 Cup of white wine
- 3 Cup of beef broth
- 2 dried bay leaves
- 1 tbsp dried Greek oregano
- 4 sprigs of thyme
- 3 sprigs rosemary
- 2 tbsp cornstarch

Instructions

- ✓ Heat the oven to 325°F.

For the Lamb Shanks:

1. Place the lamb shanks on a workspace and blot the paper towel moisture.
2. Combine garlic powder, onion powder, cumin, paprika, cinnamon, and pepper. Sprinkle kindly the lamb shanks and rub the top.
3. Heat the oil in a oven or large pot. Sear on either foot, 2-3 minutes. Set aside on a plate.

4. Stir in the onion and simmer until tender, then add the garlic. Add lemons, wine and soup. Toss out leaves and oregano. Tie your choice of herbs together and placed in the pot.
5. Back to pork steaks. The liquid should cover the shanks and then more broth or water should be applied. Cook the beef until it is very tender, 2 1/2 to 3 Hrs.
6. When the lamb shanks are tender, transfer them carefully to a plate and cover with foil to stay warm.

To Make the Sauce:

1. Remove and discard the string of remaining spices, strain the cooking liquids into a casserole through a fine-mesh strainer, press the vegetables with a spoon back.
2. Discard solids in the strainer with spoon, extract as much fat as possible from liquid bottom.
3. Return the liquid to medium-high heat. Bring liquids to a boil and cook for two cups. Five-to-10 minutes.
4. Combine cornstarch with 1/4 cup cold water in a small dish, stirring until smooth. Whisk in the braising sauce and boil until thickened.
5. Serve lamb shanks with chopped parsley in individual shallow bowls on top of mashed potato mounds.
6. Transfer the sauce to a lamb shanks serving pitcher or plate.

Cook's Note

If you choose not to use wine, substitute beef broth or chicken broth.

5. CUMIN LAMB SKEWERS

Prep Time: 20 mins

Cook Time: 08 mins

Total Time: 28 mins

Ingredients

- 1 lb boneless lamb shoulder
- Ground cumin and chili powder mix
- Bamboo skewers

SPICE MARINADE:

- 1/3 Cup of peanut oil
- 2 tbsp tbsp ground cumin
- 2/3 tbsp chili powder
- 1 tbsp Spice Mix, ground: coriander, cumin and fennel seeds powder
- 1/4-1/2 tsp Szechuan peppercorns
- 2/3 tsp salt
- 2 tsp garlic powder

Instructions

1. Prepare Marinade Spice. Mix all Spice Marinade ingredients in a bowl. Marinate cubes for 2 Hrs or overnight. Thread marinated cubes on skewers.
2. Preheat grill 10 minutes. Set skewers on the grill shelf. Grill lamb skewers on either side for 3-4 minutes, or until fully cooked. Remove skewers from barbecue. Dust the lamb skewers with spice blend and beer and salad ready to eat.

Cook's Note

For Spice Mix, you need 1 tbspful in all, mixing cumin, coriander and fennel. The ratio is yours. I used 1 part of cumin, 1/2 part of coriander and 1/2 part of fennel for this recipe.

6. SPICED LAMB KEBABS

Prep Time: 10 mins

Cook Time: 20 mins

Serves: 04 People

Ingredients

- 450g lean boneless lamb leg steaks, neck fillet or shoulder
- 3 peeled and crushed garlic cloves
- 2 tsp ground cinnamon
- 2 tsp ground cumin
- 2 tsp rapeseed
- Zest and juice of 1 lemon

Instructions

1. Place the lamb in a large bowl. Add remaining ingredients and stir to coat.
2. Fasten the lamb on 8 small or 4 wide metal or wooden skewers, and transfer to a large plate or foil-lined tray.
3. Cook on a prepared barbecue for 6-8 minutes on either side or before any meat juice runs free.
4. Serve with a couscous and chickpea salad and a lemon dressing.

Cook's Note

Instead of using a ready-made dry rub mix to replace spices.

7. GREEK LAMB SOUVLAKI SKEWERS

Prep Time: 15 mins (+30 mins to Marinate)

Cook Time: 16 mins

Yield: 06 Skewers

Ingredients

- 1 lb. lamb leg or shoulder
- 1/3 Cup of divided olive oil
- 1 tbsp freshly squeezed lemon juice
- 2 tbsp minced garlic
- 2 tbsp Italian seasoning
- 1 tbsp cumin powder
- 2 tbsp salt
- 1 tbsp ground black pepper

Instructions

1. Marinate the lamb. Add 1/4 cup of lemon juice, olive oil,, minced garlic, Italian seasoning, cumin, salt and pepper. Press out the air and close securely. Press the lamb marinade to coat. Marinate for 30 minutes to an overnight, infuse all ingredients into the beef.
2. Skewer's lamb. Thread the lamb and sprinkle some olive oil gently.
3. Skewers barbecue. Heat a skillet over medium heat for 4-5 minutes and rub oil into the pan. You should note the hot and ready oil shimmer and sizzle. Grill on either side for 8-10 minutes or until the lamb's internal temperature reaches 155 F. Cook 1-2 more minutes on either side or before the internal temperature crosses 160 F.

Cook's Note

Equipment used: skewers, barbecue tongs, indoor grill pan, automated meat thermometer.

Marinate the lamb. Letting the lamb marinate for at least 30 minutes is vital to encourage the flavors to infuse and get juicier. Marinade lemon juice also helps tenderize the lamb. I like to let it marinate overnight, if you have time.

Nutrition Facts

Total Fat 23.7g, Cholesterol 51.5mg, Sodium 2371.4mg, Total Carbohydrate 3g, Sugars 0.2g.

8. GREEK LAMB SOUVLAKIS

Prep Time: 15 mins

Marinate Time: 01-02 Hrs

Cook Time: 20 mins

Ingredients

For Lamb Skewers:

- 1 1/2 lbs lamb chops
- 1/4 cup of red onion diced
- 2 minced cloves garlic
- Juice of 1 lemon
- 1/4 Cup of red wine vinegar
- 1/4 Cup of olive oil
- 1/2 tsp kosher salt
- 1 tsp coarsely cracked black pepper
- 1 tbsp dried oregano

For Pitas:

- 4 whole-grain pitas
- 1/4 cup of red onion sliced
- 1/4 Cup of crumbled feta cheese
- 1/2 Cup of tzatziki sauce
- Fresh dill for garnish

Instructions

1. Cut lamb chops into 1-inch cubes and placed them in a container. Add onion, garlic, lemon juice, vinegar, oil, salt, pepper and oregano. Remove to blend and shield. Let lamb marinate in fridge 1-2 Hrs.
2. Heat to medium-high heat. Skewer on metal skewers or wooden skewers. Grill lamb skewers up, revolving every few minutes, until pink in the middle, about 8-10 minutes.
3. Heat pitas on the grill until warm, but soft and pliable. Top lamb, cabbage, feta, tzatziki and fresh dill. Enjoy it!

9. CLASSIC RACK OF LAMB

Prep Time: 10 mins

Cook Time: 25 mins

Marinating Time: 1 1/2 Hrs to Overnight

Yield: 1 Rack Serves 2 or 3 People

Ingredients

- 1 1/4 to 2 pounds for every rack
- For each rib rack:
- 2 tsp chopped fresh rosemary
- 1 tsp chopped fresh thyme
- 2 minced cloves garlic
- Salt & Pepper
- 2 tbsp extra virgin olive oil

Instructions

1. Brush rib rack with rosemary, thyme and garlic mixture all over. Sprinkle with fresh black pepper. Place in a heavy plastic oil bag.
2. Pour oil out, coating the lamb rack. Squeeze the bag and close as much air as you can. Place in a container to trap the leak if the bag leaks.
3. Marinate overnight or at room temperature for 1 1/2 to 2 Hrs as the lamb approaches room temperature in the next step.
4. Get lamb to room temp: remove lamb rack from the refrigerator for 1 1/2 to 2 Hrs before cooking for room temp.
5. Heat oven to 450°F. Place oven rack, so the lamb is in the center of oven.
6. Score the fat, sprinkle with salt & pepper, wrap bones in foil, place fat side up in pan: score the fat, make deep shallow cuts into the fat, spaced about an inch apart.
7. Sprinkle the rack with salt and pepper. Place the bone lamb rack on a roasting pan lined with foil. Wrap the uncovered rib bones in a foil so they don't smoke.
8. Roast at high heat to brown, then reduce heat to finish: place the roast at 450°F for 10 minutes or until the roast surface is well browned.
9. Then drop heat to 300°F. Cook 10-20 minutes longer before a meat thermometer is placed into the thickest section of meat 125°F on a medium-rare or 135°F. Add from the oven and cover with foil for 15 mins.
10. Cut lamb chops off the rack by slicing between bones. Serve 2-3 chops a human.

10. ROAST LAMB

Yield: 08 to 12 Servings

Time About: 03 Hrs

Ingredients

- 1 large lamb roast: semiboneless leg, boneless butterflied leg, bone-in shoulder or double loin
- 3 tbsp Dijon mustard
- Leaves from 6 fresh rosemary sprigs + extra sprigs and branches for garnish
- 6 smashed and peeled garlic cloves
- 4 ounces softened unsalted butter
- Black pepper
- 1 lemon, cut in half
- 1 ¾ Cup of white wine + extra for gravy

Instructions

1. Heat the oven to 425F. Using a small sharp knife to make about a dozen incisions, each about 2 inches long, into the fat covering the meat layer.
2. Mix 2/3 anchovies, rosemary leaves and garlic cloves into a chunky paste using a mortar and pestle or blender. Using your fingers, paste directly through incisions.
3. Mix leftover anchovies with butter in paste. Smear this mixture over roast surface. Season with black pepper. Insert the lamb into a roasting pan, placing the fat side up. Pour the roast wine into the pan.
4. Reduce heat to 350 degrees and roast before internal temperature exceeds 130-135 degrees, another 60-90 minutes.
5. Baste the wine in the pan every 20 minutes or so, adding more wine if required to prevent the liquid from scorching. If necessary, use convection or broiler on the roast for the last 15 minutes of cooking.
6. Turn the pan out of the oven, remove the rack from the pan, and place the roast in a warm place, tenting with foil. Internal temperature will rise to 140-145 degrees.
7. To make sauce, scrape a few tbsp of fat by tipping the pan and spooning off the top layer. Place the pan over medium heat before simmer. Taste the simmering liquid and swirl 1/4 cup at a time with more wine until consistency and taste are right. Let the mixture not get syrupy: it should be a sharp juice, not a thick gravy.
8. Carve lamb into 1/2-inch thick slices and place with rosemary sprigs on a hot dish. Serve with hot-gravy piping.

Nutrition Facts

Calories: 107 g, fat: 56 g, carbohydrates: 0 grams dietary fiber: 1 gram sugars: 11 grams protein: 258 milligrams sodium.

11. ROASTED RACK OF LAMB

Prep & Cook Time: 20 mins + 20 mins

Servings: 04

Ingredients

- ½ Cup of fresh bread crumbs
- 2 tbsp minced garlic
- 2 tbsp chopped fresh rosemary
- ¼ tsp black pepper
- 2 tbsp olive oil
- 1 trimmed and frenched rack of lamb
- 1 tsp salt
- 1 tsp black pepper
- 2 tbsp olive oil
- 1 tbsp Dijon mustard

Instructions

1. Heat the oven to 450F. Shift the rack to the middle position.
2. Combine bread crumbs, ginger, rosemary, 1 tsp salt and 1/4 tsp pepper. Mixture in 2 tbsp of olive oil. Set aside.
3. Season the rack with salt and pepper. Heat 2 tbsp olive oil in a heavy-skillet. Sear lamb rack on both sides 1-2 minutes. Place aside a few minutes. Rub lamb rack with mustard. Roll in crumb mixture until uniformly covered. Cover bones with foil to avoid charring.
4. Arrange the hand in the skillet. Cook the lamb for 12 to 18 minutes. Let the meat hang in the meat center for 10-12 minutes and then take a meat thermometer reading. Rest 5 to 7 minutes, loosely exposed, before carving between ribs.

Cook's Note

Enable 5 to 10 degrees lower internal temperature than you want since the meat can continue to cook as it rests. Bloody rare: 115-125 degrees F Rare: 125-130 degrees F Rare: 130-140 degrees F Medium: 140-150 F.

12. BARBECUED MARINATED LAMB LEG

Prep Time: 4 Hrs 10 mins

Cook Time: 30 mins

Servings: 04

Ingredients

- 5 crushed garlic cloves
- 1 tbsp paprika
- 1 large lemon juiced
- 1/4 cup of olive oil
- 1.5 kg boned lamb leg, butterflied
- Olive oil cooking spray
- jacket potatoes, to serve

GREEN OLIVE MAYONNAISE:

- 3/4 cup of whole-egg mayonnaise
- 1/2 cup of chopped stuffed green olives
- 1 tsp paprika
- 1/2 small lemon juiced

Instructions

1. In a big, shallow ceramic bowl, combine the garlic, paprika, 2 tbsp of lemon juice, and oil. Season the lamb on both ends with salt and pepper.
2. Lambskin ranking. In the marinade, place the lamb and turn the coat over. For 3 hours, cover and refrigerate. Remove 30 minutes before cooking from the refrigerator.
3. Make mayonnaise with green olive: Meanwhile, in a bowl, mix mayonnaise, olive, paprika, and 1 tbsp of lemon juice. With salt and pepper, season. Mix thoroughly. Cover when ready to eat, then refrigerate.
4. Spray with oil on a frozen barbecue plate or a grill. High temperature. Lower the heat to medium-high heat. Lamb barbecue, skin side down, for 10 minutes. Turn it over and simmer for 5 minutes. Reduce to medium-low heat. Lamb mask, barbecue hood. For medium or before it has been cooked to your taste, barbecue for another 15 mins.
5. Withdraw from the heat. With foil, cover loosely. Place aside for 10 mins to relax in a warm spot. Thinly sliced the lamb through the grain.

13. ROSEMARY LAMB SHANKS BRAISED IN RED WINE

Prep & Cook Time: 10 mins + 01 hrs 45 mins

Cook Time: 01 hrs 45 mins

Servings: 04

Ingredients

- 4 french trimmed lamb shanks
- 2 coarsely chopped brown onions
- 2 crushed garlic cloves
- 2 cup of dry red wine
- 2 x 400g cans diced tomatoes
- 2 tbsp rosemary sprigs & 1 tbsp olive oil
- 4 cups of Massel chicken style liquid stock
- 1 cup of cornmeal
- 1/2 cup of finely grated parmesan
- 1/2 cup of mascarpone

Instructions

1. Heat the oven to 160°C. In a large flame-proof casserole bowl, heat the oil over high heat. Add half of the lamb and roast, rotating, for 5 minutes or until everything is brown.
2. Transfer to a pan. Repeat for the lamb that remains. Add the garlic & onion to the pan and cook for 5 minutes, stirring, or until the onion is tender. Put the lamb back in and spill it over the red wine. Just get it to a boil.
3. Cook for 2-3 mins the wine has halved. Withdraw from the heat. Add the rosemary and tomatoes. Bake for 1 1/2 hours, wrapped, or until the lamb almost falls off the bone.
4. To generate the polenta, heat the stock in a large saucepan over high heat.
5. Just get it to a boil. Add the cornmeal in a small, steady stream when stirring with a balloon whisk.
6. Cook for 5 mins, stirring with a wooden spoon, or until the polenta thickens and cooks. Withdraw from the heat. Add the mascarpone and parmesan and stir to blend.
7. Spoon the polenta into plates, cover, and serve with lamb.

14. LAMB AND EGGPLANT PIES

Prep Time: 15 mins

Cook Time: 50 mins

Servings: 04

Ingredients

- 1 medium eggplant, cut into twelve 1cm-thick slices
- Olive oil spray
- 400g Desiree potatoes, peeled, coarsely chopped
- 80 ml Carnation Light & Creamy Evaporated Milk
- 1 finely chopped brown onion,
- 1 zucchini, finely chopped
- 1 carrot, finely chopped, peeled
- 2 crushed garlic cloves
- 1 tsp ground allspice
- 350g lean lamb mince
- 80ml red wine
- 400g can no-added-salt chopped tomatoes
- Steamed green round beans, to serve

Instructions

1. Heat a high barbecue. Spray the oil with the eggplant. Cook each side for 2-3 mins charred and tender.
2. Cook the potato for 15 minutes in a large saucepan of boiling water or until tender. Uh, drain. Moving back to the pan. Add milk that has evaporated. Mash through until smooth.
3. Meanwhile, over low heat, heat a saucepan. Use oil to mist. Stir-cook the onion, zucchini, and carrot for 5 minutes or until tender. Add allspice and garlic. Cook, stirring, for around 1 min or until fragrant.
4. Add the mince and cook, stirring with a wooden spoon to separate any lumps, for 5 minutes or until the color changes. Add a wine. Simmer until half the sum is reduced. Add the tomato mixture. Reduce heat to low levels. Simmer for 10 mins there is a dense mixture.
5. Heat the oven to 180 degrees C. Spray four ovenproof ramekins with an oil volume of 250ml. Place each dish with 1 slice of eggplant. Cover with a combination of 2 teaspoons of mince. Continue to cover with the remaining mix of eggplant and mince. Top of the potato. Bake until golden for 20 mins or until golden. Serve along with the beans.

15. GREEK LAMB WITH WATERMELON SALAD

Prep Time: 02 Hrs 20 mins

Cook Time: 15 mins

Servings: 04

Ingredients

- 2 tsp cumin seeds
- 2 tbsp fresh rosemary
- 1 tsp whole black peppercorns
- 1/2 tsp dried chili flakes
- Grated zest of 1 lemon & 1 orange
- 100ml extra virgin olive oil
- 800g trimmed lamb backstraps
- 1/4 cup of chopped mint leaves
- 1/3 cup of Greek Style Yoghurt

WATERMELON SALAD:

- 1 tbsp olive oil
- 1 tbsp lemon juice
- 300g roughly chopped watermelon flesh
- 120g feta, crumbled
- 1/2 cup of mint leaves
- 1/2 cup of pitted kalamata olives

Instructions

1. In a mortar and pestle, pound cumin, rosemary, peppercorns, chili, and 1 teaspoon salt until coarsely ground. Apply the lemon zest and orange to the mixture and mix in the oil. In a shallow dish, place the lamb, pour over the marinade, and turn to coat well. For 2 hours, cover and refrigerate.
2. Heat the furnace to 200°C. Over medium to high heat, heat a heavy-based frypan. Sear the lamb on both sides in 2 batches, rotating, for 2-3 mins. Transfer the lamb to a baking dish, then roast in the oven for a medium-rare duration of 7 minutes or until cooked to your taste. Set aside for 5 mins to relax.
3. Meanwhile, whisk the oil and lemon juice together for the watermelon salad, then season and toss the remaining ingredients in a large bowl.
4. Stir in the yogurt with the mint and season well. Cut the lamb backstraps and serve on the side with the watermelon salad and minted yogurt.

16. LAMB SEPT-HEURES

Prep Time: 15 mins

Cook Time: 07 Hrs 40 mins

Servings: 06

Ingredients

- 1 tbsp olive oil
- 2.5kg excess fat trimmed leg of lamb
- 2 thickly sliced brown onions
- 1 head garlic, broken into cloves, unpeeled
- 2 bunches of baby carrots, trimmed, scrubbed
- 500ml white wine
- 500ml Massel chicken style liquid stock
- 1/3 bunch fresh thyme
- 4 dried bay leaves

Instructions

1. Warmth the oil in a huge flameproof cooking container over high warmth. The Season's Lamb. Cook until golden, rotating, or for 8 minutes. Transfer to a saucepan. Cook the onion until soft, or for 2 mins, stirring continuously. Remove it from the heat.
2. Heat the 110-degree cup oven. In the pan, set the lamb. Place the lamb and the carrots around the garlic. Add the wine, stock, thyme, and bay leaves. Cover loosely with foil. Bake for 7 hours, sometimes basting.
3. Transfer to a tray with the carrots and lamb. Keep wet, just. Discard the thyme and bay leaves. The onion is transferred to a processor for fruit. Squeeze through the garlic cloves and discard the flesh. Until the operation is smooth. Skim the fat off the oil's peak point.
4. Add the onion mixture to the gasoline. Get the high-medium heat to a boil. Simmer for 30 minutes or before it cuts the total by half. Serve with lamb and carrots.

17. LAMB & SPINACH PASTA

Prep Time: 20 mins

Cook Time: 10 mins

Servings: 04

Ingredients

- 300g dried pappardelle pasta
- 350g lamb leg steaks
- Olive oil spray
- 1 tbsp olive oil
- 2 crushed garlic cloves
- 3 tsp finely grated lemon rind
- 300g baby spinach leaves
- 1 tbsp water
- 35g toasted flaked almonds
- 60ml fresh lemon juice
- Extra virgin olive oil, to serve

Instructions

1. Cook the pasta in an enormous pot of salted bubbling water until still somewhat firm. Drain, uh.
2. Meanwhile, season all the sides of the lamb with salt and pepper and spray them with oil. The High Barbecue Heat. Cook the lamb for 2-3 mins on either side, medium, or until cooked to your liking. Transfer to a saucepan. Cover with foil and put in a safe spot for 5 mins to unwind.
3. When the lamb is sleeping, heat the oil in a non-stick frying pan over medium heat. Garlic, rind with lemon, spinach, and water are added. Cook for 1 min the spinach is just wilting.
4. Thinly sliced the lamb. For the lamb, spinach mixture, and almonds, add the pasta and toss to combine. Pour over the mixture with lemon juice and season with salt and pepper. Drizzle with olive oil and balance appropriately.

18. PORCINI-CRUSTED LAMB WITH MINTED PEA MASH

Prep Time: 25 mins

Cook Time: 25 mins

Servings: 04

Ingredients

- 2 1/2 cups of frozen peas
- 1/2 cup of chopped mint leaves
- 30g unsalted butter
- 20g dried porcini mushrooms
- 1/3 cup of plain flour
- 8 large French-trimmed lamb cutlets
- 1 lightly beaten egg
- 4 sprigs vine-ripened cherry tomatoes
- 1/4 cup of olive oil
- 1 tbsp balsamic vinegar

Instructions

1. Cook peas in bubbling water for 2 to 3 mins. Drain, Process half the Peas and mint and butter until soft, then return to the pan and season all the peas. Cover and set aside.
2. Heat the oven to 180C. In a processor or coffee grinder, grind the porcini and the flour into a powder. Season, place on a tray, next. Dip the lamb in the milk, then coat the pasta with porcini.
3. Warmth the oil over medium warmth in an enormous skillet. Brown lamb in batches, for 2 mins on each side. Place them in a tomato roasting pan. Roast for 5 minutes until it is medium-rare for lamb and mild for tomatoes.
4. When you reheat the mash, rest for 5 minutes. Place mash on plates, then top with tomatoes and lamb. Mix the balsamic juice in the bowl, then drizzle over it.

19. VEGETABLE COUSCOUS WITH SPICED LAMB

Prep Time: 10 mins

Cook Time: 15 mins

Servings: 04

Ingredients

- 3 tsp McCormick Middle Eastern spices
- 2 (about 400g) lamb eye of loin

1/2 cup of chopped continental parsley

- 2 tsp olive oil
- 290g couscous
- 1 tbsp coarsely grated lemon rind
- 310ml Massel salt reduced chicken style liquid stock
- 60ml fresh lemon juice
- 340g chargrilled capsicum
- 1 x 280g btl artichoke hearts, drained, halved
- 130g Greek-style natural yogurt

Instructions

1. On a pan, place the spice blend. Add the lamb, and turn the coat over. Warmth the oil over medium to high warmth in a non-stick griddle.
2. Add the lamb and reduce to medium heat. Cook on each side for 3-4 mins, medium or until cooked to your taste. Transfer to a pan. Cover with foil loosely and set aside to rest for 5 mins. Slice through the grain thickly.
3. Meanwhile, in a medium heatproof bowl, place the couscous and lemon rind. In a small saucepan, bring the stock to a boil. Over the couscous, pour in the stock and lemon juice.
4. Cover and set aside for 3-4 minutes or until you have consumed all the oil. Separate the grains with a fork. Add the capsicum, parsley, and artichoke and mix until well mixed.
5. Divide between serving plates the couscous mixture. To serve, top with lamb and a dollop of yogurt.

20. LEFTOVER LAMB RAGU

Prep Time: 05 mins

Cook Time: 25 mins

Servings: 04 people

Ingredients

- 2 tbsp olive oil
- 1 diced finely onion
- 1 diced finely carrot
- 1 diced finely stick of celery
- 3 cloves garlic crushed
- 600 g cooked lamb leftovers chopped
- 350 ml passata
- 300 ml lamb stock
- 3 dried bay leaves
- Salt and pepper
- 250 g pappardelle
- Parmesan to serve

Instructions

1. In a big saucepan or sauté pan, place the olive oil, onion, carrot, and celery and cook over gentle heat with a lid on for 5 mins until softened. Occasionally stir.
2. Add the garlic and lamb and simmer over low heat for a further 2 mins.
3. Passata, lamb stock, bay leaves, salt, and pepper are all added. Turn the heat up, and get it to a boil.
4. Reduce heat and boil until the sauce is nicely thickened for 15 mins.
5. Meanwhile, according to box directions, cook your pasta and rinse, reserving a little boiling water.
6. When the sauce is finished, throw the pappardelle in the sauce along with some of the boiling water and serve with parmesan cheese to rub on top, if you like.

Cook's Note

Data on diet are approximate and only meant as a reference.

21. LAMB CHOPS WITH BALSAMIC REDUCTION

Prep Time: 10 mins

Cook Time: 15 mins

Servings: 04

Ingredients

- ¾ tsp dried rosemary
- ¼ tsp dried basil
- ½ tsp dried thyme
- Salt and pepper as need
- 4 lamb chops
- 1 tbsp olive oil
- ¼ cup of minced shallots
- ⅓ cup of aged balsamic vinegar
- ¾ cup of chicken broth
- 1 tbsp butter

Instructions

1. Mix the rosemary, basil, thyme, salt, and pepper in a little bowl or cup. On both ends, brush this paste onto the lamb chops. Place them on a pan, cover, and set aside to absorb the flavors for 15 mins.
2. Heat the olive oil and over medium heat in a skillet. Place the lamb chops in the skillet and cook on medium rare for around 3 1/2 mins per hand, or continue to cook to your preferred doneness. Remove from the skillet, and on a serving platter, stay warm.
3. Add the shallots to the skillet and roast, only until browned, for a few minutes. Stir in the vinegar, scrape from the bottom of the pan some pieces of lamb, then stir in the chicken broth.
4. Continue to cook and stir for around 5 mins over medium-high heat, until the sauce has halved. If you don't, it'll be runny and not good with the sauce. Remove and stir in the butter from the heat. Pour over the chops of beef, and serve.

1. SPICY GINGER CASHEW PORK

Prep Time: 05 mins

Cook Time: 20 mins

Additional Time: 05 mins

Ingredients

FOR THE SAUCE:

- 1/3 Cup of homemade spicy sweet chili sauce
- 1/4 Cup of low-sodium tamari
- Juice of 1 medium lime

FOR THE STIR-FRY:

- 2-1/2 tsp toasted sesame oil
- 2 tsp grated fresh ginger
- 3 cloves minced fresh garlic
- Peanut or Coconut oil for frying
- 1-1/4 to 1-1/2 pounds top boneless loin sliced thin pork chop
- 3 tbsp cornstarch
- 1/2 tsp white pepper
- 1/2 to 3/4 Cup of roasted unsalted

FOR SERVING:

- Cooked rice or cauliflower rice
- Crushed red pepper flakes
- Sliced green onions
- Torn cilantro leaves

Instructions

1. Combine the chili sauce, tamari and lime juice in a shallow cup.
2. Cut pork with cornstarch and white pepper.
3. Heat a skillet and cook the garlic and ginger for around 30 seconds on medium-high heat. Then work in batches stir-fry pork in batches, adding more coconut oil if needed until the pork is fried and crispy.
4. Transfer the pork to a clean pan, replicate the remaining slices.

5. Wipe your paper towel wok and minimize heat to mild. Add cashews and stir-fry toasted spots. Transfer the toasted cashews to pork plate.
6. Load the sauce into the wok and simmer. Then throw in the pork and cashews before the sauce sticks and caramelizes to the crispy pork and cashews.
7. Serve with rice, green onions, red pepper flakes and cilantro.

2. ASIAN PORK SATAY

Marinade Time: 05 mins

Cook Time: 20 mins

Ingredients

FOR THE PORK SATAY, SIMMER:

- 1 jar hoisin sauce
- ½ Cup of chili garlic sauce
- ¼ Cup of honey
- ¼ Cup of rice vinegar
- 2 Tbsp. toasted sesame oil Salt as need
- 1 trimmed pork tenderloin

FOR THE RICE, BOIL:

- 2 Cup of water pinch of salt
- 1 Cup of dry medium grain rice
- ½ Cup of frozen green peas
- 2 tbsp rice vinegar

Instructions

1. Heat grill to medium-high heat. Brush grill with grease.
2. Bring hoisin, chili garlic sauce, butter, vinegar, and oil to a boil. Cook the marinade, season with salt, and set aside to cool.
3. Prepare pork, cut it into thirds first, then make 6 bits in half crosswise. Slice each section in half lengthwise to produce 12 strips, each 4- to 6-inch long. Toss marinade pork strips, then string strips on skewers.
4. Make a tea and pour it over your head. Add rice, cover, boil for 15 minutes. Take off sun. Stir in peas and vinegar.
5. Arrange satay on the grill to protect the skewers and cook for 3–4 minutes. Flip satay, baste with marinade, then grill for 3–4 minutes. Serve with Cucumber Salad

3. ASAIN BBQ PORK KABOBS

Prep Time: 20 mins

Cook Time: 12 mins

Servings: 04 People

Ingredients

- 1 pork tenderloin
- 1/2 Cup of ketchup
- 1/2 Cup of vegetable oil
- 1/2 Cup of soy sauce
- 1/2 Cup of brown sugar
- 1/4 Cup of apple cider vinegar
- 1/4 Cup of Thai sweet chili sauce
- 2 minced cloves garlic
- 1 sliced bunch scallions
- 2 tsp coarse black pepper

Instructions

1. In a gallon-sized zip-top container, mix all marinade ingredients.
2. Trim any extra silver skin or fat outside the tenderloin. Cut the tenderloin into cubes. Aim to get them as big as possible.
3. Place the cubed pork in the marinade, close the bag firmly, and toss to marinate each piece of meat. Set the bag on a tray and refrigerate for 8 Hrs or up to 24 Hrs.
4. Remove pork parts from the bag, shake off any big pieces of onion and marinade.
5. Pour the leftover marinade into a medium saucepan and boil. Cook the skewers at a rolling boil for 5-10 minutes. Remove from fire, cut into two bowls. One for grilling your pork and one for serving your pork when done frying.
6. Slide marinated pork onto 4 skewers.
7. Heat your barbecue to 400°F. You'll barbecue over clear fire, which means over the flames on your grill.
8. Cook the kabobs on the grill for 10-12 minutes, baste with your reduced marinade sauce and turn every 3-4 minutes, or until the internal meat temperature reads 145F and the pork edges are crispy and caramelized.
9. Serve with the leftover sauce.!

4. POTATO AND PORK SKILLET

Prep/Total Time: 20 mins

Makes: 04 Servings

Ingredients

- 4 boneless pork loin chops
- 1/4 tsp pepper
- 1 tbsp olive oil
- 4 thinly sliced medium red potatoes
- 1 sliced medium onion
- 1 tsp dried oregano
- 1 Cup of chicken broth
- 1/2 Cup of diced roasted sweet red peppers

Instructions

1. Sprinkle peppered pork chops. Cook chops in oil over medium heat on each side for 2-3 minutes or until chops are lightly browned: rinse. Remove, warm-up.
2. Saute the potatoes, onion, and oregano for 6-8 minutes or until potatoes are almost tender. Bring broth and red peppers to a boil.
3. Top pork chops. Reduce heat: cover and simmer for 4-6 minutes or until 145° read, stirring periodically. Let stand five minutes before serving.

5. PORK SATAY WITH PEANUT SAUCE

Prep Time: 15 mins

Cook Time: 15 mins

Servings: 02 Persons

Ingredients

- 1 pound pork chops cut into 1-inch cubes
- 2 minced garlic cloves
- 1 tbsp fresh ginger grated
- 2 tsp chili paste
- 2-3 tbsp sweet soy sauce
- 2 tbsp vegetable oil
- 1 finely chopped shallot
- 1 tsp ground coriander

- ½ Cup of coconut milk
- 4 ounces unsalted butter

Instructions

1. Mix half the garlic with the ginger, 1 tsp spicy pepper sauce, 1 tbsp soy sauce and 1 tbsp oil. Connect meat to mixture and marinate for 15 minutes.
2. Preheat the fryer to 380F. Place the marinated meat in the basket for 12 minutes until brown and done. Turn while cooking.
3. Meanwhile, sauce peanut. Heat 1 tbsp. of oil in a saucepan and sauté gently with garlic. Add the coriander and cook 1-2 minutes. Mix coconut milk and peanuts with 1 tsp hot pepper sauce and 1 tbsp soy sauce with shallot mixture and cook gently for 5 minutes, stirring continuously.
4. Serve the beef with gravy!

6. PORK SKEWERS WITH COUSCOUS SALAD

Hands-On Time: 25 mins

Total Time: 01 hr 30 mins

Servings: 04

Ingredients

- 1 pound pork tenderloin
- 1 peeled and chopped shallot
- 2 peeled and halved cloves garlic
- ¼ Cup of lime juice
- 1 tsp garam masala
- 1 tsp chili powder
- 1 ½ tsp ground turmeric
- 1 tsp fine sea salt
- 1 Cup of low-sodium chicken stock or vegetable
- 4 tsp + 1 tbsp olive oil
- 1 Cup of couscous
- 2 thinly sliced shallots
- 2 tbsp cashews
- ¼ Cup of dried tart cherries
- 1 1-inch piece peeled and julienned resh ginger
- 1 Cup of packed arugula leaves
- ½ Cup of crumbled feta
- Lime wedges

Instructions

1. Placed pork in a bowl. In a small food processor, pulse shallot, 2 Tbsp. Lime juice, garam masala, chili powder, 1/2 tsp turmeric, 1/2 tsp salt: sprinkle over pork. Toss coat. Chill, 1 Hr covered.
2. Thread pork on eight bamboo skewers. Grill on a wrapped grill rack directly over medium coals 4-6 minutes or until beef is only slightly pink in the middle, rotating once.
3. Meanwhile, carry stock to a rolling boil with remaining salt and 1 tsp. Olive olive oil. Upon boiling stock, stir in couscous: remove from fire. Let stand 8-10 minutes or until couscous is tender. Fluffing with a fork.
4. Heat 2 tsp in medium saucepan. Medium-high olive oil. Add sliced shallots: cook 3-4 minutes or until light brown. Add cashews, cherries, ginger, and turmeric. Cook 2 to 3 mins and slightly seared.
5. Cooked couscous with shallot mixture in a large mixing bowl. Arugula and feta fold. Remaining lime juice. Season with salt and black pepper. Transfer to a tray. Top skewered pork. Drizzle 1 tbsp. Olive olive oil. Serve with lime coins.

Nutrition Facts

Per Serving: 503 calories: total fat 17g: cholesterol 90mg: sodium 1060mg: potassium 680mg: carbohydrates 53g: fiber 4g: sugar 10g: protein 34g: trans fatty acid 0g: calcium 142mg: iron 3mg.

7. TUSCAN PORK KEBABS

Prep Time: 15 mins

Cook Time: 15 mins

Yield: 04 Servings

Ingredients

- 4 tsp olive oil
- 1 tbsp grated lemon rind
- ½ tsp salt
- ½ tsp freshly ground black pepper
- 2 crushed garlic cloves
- 1 pound pork tenderloin, trimmed
- 16 pieces red bell pepper
- 16 pieces yellow bell pepper

Instructions

1. Prepare medium-high barbecue.
2. Combine olive oil, lemon rind, salt, pepper, and garlic in a large bowl, stirring well. Marinate at room temperature 15 minutes, tossing sometimes.
3. Thread pork and bell peppers on any of 8 skewers. Place skewers on a grill rack covered with spray: grill 10 minutes or until pork is cooked, turning periodically.
4. Heat a large skillet over medium-high heat. Add 1 tbsp olive oil and coat. Apply 8 cups of chopped Swiss chard, 2 tablespoons of garlic, and 1/8 teaspoon of salt: saute for 5 minutes or until chard wilts.

Nutrition Facts

198 calories: fat 8.8g: protein 24.7g: carbohydrates 4.5g: cholesterol 67mg: iron 1.6mg: sodium 346mg: calcium 15mg.

---

8. MUSHROOM PORK CHOPS

Prep Time: 15 mins

Cook Time: 02 Hrs 06 mins

Servings: 04 People

Ingredients

- 2 pounds thick pork chops
- Salt & pepper as need
- ⅔ Cup of panko bread crumbs
- ⅔ Cup of seasoned bread crumbs
- 2 tbsp divided fresh parsley
- 1 tsp garlic powder
- 2 eggs beaten
- 1 tbsp oil for browning
- 8 ounces mushrooms
- 2 cans condensed mushroom soup

Instructions

1. Heat the oven to 350°F.
2. Test bone or residue pork chops. Salt & pepper season.
3. Combine panko crumbs, seasoned crumbs, 1 1/2 tsp of garlic powder & parsley.
4. Beat eggs and mix them with crumbs.
5. Heat 1 tbsp of oil and add pork chops. Brown on both ends, approximately 3 minutes. If required, repeat with remaining pork chops adding more oil.
6. Place pork chops in a big bakery. Sliced mushrooms and mushroom broth.
7. Bake 1 1/2 to 2 hrs, pull back and inspect one of the pork chops. It should be tender fork. If not, bake 20-30 minutes.
8. Garnish with parsley over mashed potatoes.

Cook's Note

Using blade chop, shoulder chop, sirloin chop or steak.

In this recipe, lean pork chops won't fit well, you want something marbled with more fat for better results.

You should make your own fluffy mushroom sauce instead of the canned mushroom broth, or top this casserole.

If your pork's tough, it usually needs more time. Place in the oven for 20 mins.

9. PORK AND MUSHROOM RICE BAKE

Prep & Cook Time: 45 mins

Servings: 06 to 08 People

Ingredients

- 1 pounds pork tenderloin, cut into bite-sized pieces
- 1 chopped medium onion
- 1 1/4 lbs thickly sliced mushrooms
- 2 minced garlic cloves
- Kosher salt and freshly ground black pepper
- 4 tbsp melted butter
- 1 tsp dried thyme
- 1 1/2 Cup of long-grain white rice
- 1 1/2 Cup of chicken broth
- 1 1/4 Cup of water
- 2 tbsp olive oil

Instructions

1. Heat the oven to 350F. Grease a 9x13-inch baking pan with non stick spray.
2. Toss pork, mushrooms, cabbage, garlic, salt, pepper and melted butter in a medium bowl.
3. Inoa, thyme, chicken broth, and water in the prepared baking pan. Layer over pan uniformly.
4. Spread mushroom/pork mixture uniformly over rice. Drizzle with oil.
5. Bake until golden mushrooms are cooked, 35-40 minutes. Remove from the oven for 5 minutes. Remove all, serve and enjoy!

10. BAKED PORK CHOPS & RICE

Prep Time: 10 mins

Cook Time: 02 Hrs

Servings: 04 People

Ingredients

- 2 tbsp vegetable oil
- 4-5 boneless pork chops
- 1 tsp salt
- 1 tsp pepper
- 1 tsp onion powder
- 2 tsp divided dried rosemary
- 1 tsp thyme
- 1 10 ounces cream of chicken soup
- 1 10 ounces cream of mushroom soup
- 1 1/2 Cup of milk
- 1 Cup of long-grain white rice
- 1/2 Cup of butter

Instructions

1. Heat the oven to 275F.
2. Season all sides with salt, pepper, onion powder and 1 tsp rosemary.
3. Add 2 tbs of vegetable oil and brown pork chops on both sides for around 3-5 mins.
4. Add from heat in a 9"x13" pan, set aside.
5. In a medium saucepan, add mushroom soup cream, chicken soup cream, milk, remaining rosemary and thyme and whisk together until stirred, then stir in rice.

6. Add butter and place the saucepan on the stove and heat until butter is melted.
7. Pour over pork chops, cover with tin foil, bake 2 Hrs.
8. Remove from oven and parsley if necessary.

11. PORK SHAWARMA SKEWERS

Prep Time: 25 mins

Cook Time: 10 mins

Total Time: 35 mins

Ingredients

- 500g thinly sliced pork scotch fillet steaks
- 11/2 tsp mild paprika
- 1 tsp ground cumin
- 1 tsp ground coriander
- 1/2 tsp ground turmeric
- 1/2 tsp sea salt flakes
- 2 tbs olive oil + 2 tbs olive oil extra
- 200g canned lentils, drained, rinsed
- 1/2 thinly sliced small red onion
- 1 Lebanese cucumber, shaved into ribbons
- 1 baby cos lettuce, trimmed, leaves separated
- 1 tbs lemon juice
- 1 crushed small garlic clove
- 400g can chickpeas, drained, rinsed
- 1 tbs tahini
- 1/4 Cup of toasted pine nuts
- 1/4 Cup of lemon juice

Instructions

1. In a bowl, mix bacon, paprika, cumin, turmeric and salt. Thread pork on skewers. Set aside.
2. Process garlic, chickpeas, tahini, pine nuts, olive oil, lemon juice and 1/4 cup water in a food processor until smooth. Season as needed.
3. Heat 1 tbs of oil over medium-high heat in a large frying pan. Heat skewers, rotating periodically, for 8-10 minutes or until mildly charred.
4. Meanwhile, mix lentils, cabbage, cucumber, basil, remaining oil and lemon juice in a bowl. Season as needed with pork skewers and hummus.

12. GRILLED TAHINI PORK SKEWERS

Prep Time: 25 mins

Cook Time: 12 mins

Servings: 04

Ingredients

- 1/2 Cup of tahini
- 1/2 Cup of coconut milk
- 2 tbsp fish sauce
- 1 tbsp honey + more for serving
- 2 tbsp lime juice
- 1 tbsp sesame oil
- 1 3/4 pound boneless pork
- microgreens for serving
- 1 thinly sliced red bird's eye chili
- 1/3 Cup of chopped salted peanuts

Instructions

1. Combine tahini, coconut milk, fish sauce, sugar, lime juice and sesame oil in a bowl and whisk together.
2. Place the pork in another bowl and add half of the tahini mixture over the pork. Marinate pork for 15 minutes.
3. Grill to medium heat. Thread the pork on the skewers and grill for 2-3 minutes or until the pork is cooked through.
4. Serve with a little honey and micro-greens, chili and peanuts.

13. CREAMY PAPRIKA PORK

Prep/Total Time: 30 mins

Makes: 04 Servings

Ingredients

- 1 pork tenderloin, cut into 1-inch cubes
- 1 tsp all-purpose flour
- 4 tsp paprika
- 3/4 tsp salt
- 1/4 tsp pepper
- 1 tbsp butter
- 3/4 cup of heavy whipping cream
- Hot cooked egg noodles or rice

Instructions

1. Toss the flour and seasonings with the bacon. Heat butter over medium heat in a large skillet; saute the pork until lightly browned, 4-5 mins.
2. Add the milk to get the cream to a boil, stirring until the browned portions of the pan have loosened. Cook until the cream is somewhat thickened, uncovered, 5-7 minutes.
3. With pasta, serve. Sprinkle with parsley if needed.

14. APPLE AND PORK MEATBALLS RECIPE

Prep Time: 15 mins

Cook Time: 30 mins

Serves: 04

Ingredients

- 500g pack 12% fat pork mince
- 1½ Gala apples, cored & grated
- 2 crushed garlic cloves
- 5g finely chopped fresh sage leaves
- Pinch of grated nutmeg
- 2 tbsp plain flour
- 1 tbsp olive oil
- 200g tomato passata

Instructions

1. 7, 220 ° C, fan 200 ° C. Heat the oven to gas. In a bowl, placed the mince, apples, garlic, part of the salvia, nutmeg, and flour. Season and combine well.
2. Cut into 16 and then roll into balls. Place and clean the tops with olive oil in an oiled baking dish. For 15 mins, roast, then spill over the passata. Until cooked through, roast for another 10-15 mins. Stir in a bit of water if the sauce is too dry.
3. Divide between 4 plates the meatballs; scatter with the remaining sage. Delicious with mash and red cabbage served if you prefer.

15. ROAST PORK BELLY WITH SPICED PLUM SAUCE

Prep Time: 20 mins

Cook + Resting Time: 01 hrs 50 mins

Serves: 04

Ingredients

- ½ tsp fennel seeds
- ½ tsp black peppercorns
- ¼ tsp ground cinnamon
- ¼ tsp chili flakes
- 1 tsp sea salt flakes
- 800g skin scored pork belly
- 300g rice, cooked, to serve
- 250g pak choi, steamed, to serve

For the plum sauce:

- ½ finely sliced small exhalation shallot
- 250g Flavor King plums, stoned and chopped
- ½ seeded and chopped red chili
- 1 garlic clove, crushed into a paste
- 1 tbsp caster sugar
- ½ tsp soy sauce
- ½ tbsp red wine vinegar
- 1 cinnamon stick
- 1-star anise
- 2½ cm piece ginger, peeled and grated

Instructions

1. 9, 240 ° C, fan 220 ° C. Heat the oven to gas. Grind the fennel seeds and peppercorns using a pestle and mortar, then whisk in the ground cinnamon, chili flakes, and sea salt. Sprinkle over the pork's skin and rub in the markers of the score.
2. Place the pork in a hot pan on a rack and cook in the oven for 30 minutes, and turn the heat down to a 160 °C gas and add 200 ml of water to the base of the pan. Roast for another 1 hour and 20 mins, until cooked through.
3. Meanwhile, for the plum, make a gravy. In a heavy pan, place all the ingredients and cook for 5 mins, stirring, over high heat. For 8-10 minutes, place a lid on the pan and cook, stirring every so often, until the plums are thickened and almost crushed. The cinnamon stick and the star anise are separated and discarded.
4. Take the pork from the oven and leave for 10 mins to rest, wrapped. Spoon over the spicy plum sauce and serve with the pak choi and rice.

16. PORK CHOPS WITH POTATO WEDGES RECIPE

Prep Time: 10 mins

Cook Time: 40 mins

Serves: 04

Ingredients

- 6 Redmere Farms potatoes
- 1 large sliced Redmere Farms onion
- 1 tbsp vegetable oil
- Black pepper
- 2 eating Rosedene Farms apples
- 4 Woodside Farms pork chops
- 1 tsp vegetable oil
- mixed vegetables, to serve

Instructions

1. Heat the oven to 400ºF. Cut the potato into 8 wedges each. Place it with the onion in a roasting pan. Sprinkle with grease, sprinkle with chili powder and black pepper and fry for 15 minutes.
2. Core and carve the apples into rings. Place 4 pork chops on top of the apple slices in a separate pan. Brush and roast with oil for 25 minutes or cooked through. Serve with vegetables that have been blended.

17. PAPRIKA PORK FAJITAS

Prep Time: 25 mins

Cook Time: 25 mins

Serves: 04

Ingredients

For the fajitas:

- 40ml olive oil
- 500g pork tenderloin
- 1 finely sliced onion
- 1 de-seeded and finely sliced green pepper
- 1 de-seeded and finely sliced red pepper
- 1 yellow pepper
- 1tbsp paprika
- 1 tsp ground cumin
- 8 flour tortillas
- Salt & pepper
- sprigs of coriander to garnish

For the garnish:

- 150ml Tesco Healthy Eating soured cream
- 100ml Tesco light mayonnaise
- 1 minced clove garlic
- 1tsp paprika &

Instructions

1. Whisk together the garlic, mayonnaise, soaked cream, and paprika in a small mixing bowl until smooth. Begin by preparing the garnish. As required, season, then cover and chill until appropriate. Make the fajita filling by heating the olive oil in a large frying pan set over a moderate fire.
2. Saute the pork for 6-8 mins, occasionally stirring, until golden brown is full color. Add the onion and the peppers and blend well. Lower heat and cover the pot for 2-3 minutes to allow the steam to soften the pork and vegetables.
3. Remove the lid and add some seasoning, cumin, and paprika and continue cooking for 2-3 minutes before removing it from the heat. Heat another frying pan for 1 min over medium heat, then heat the flour tortillas in it on both sides for 10-15 seconds until warm. Lay the filling on a flat surface and spoon it into the middle of it.

4. Cover with a little prepared soured cream sauce, then roll up and arrange to keep them in place on plates with the seam underneath. Serve directly as a garnish with a coriander sprig.

18. STUFFING AND PORK WELLINGTON RECIPE

Serves: 08

30 mins to prepare and 01 hrs 10 mins to Cook + Cooling

Ingredients

- 1 tbsp olive oil
- 1 finely chopped onion
- 4 finely chopped garlic cloves
- 2 x 350g packs Tesco Finest sausagemeat
- 85g fresh white bread
- 50g dried cranberries, roughly chopped
- 25g roughly chopped shelled pistachios
- 15g finely chopped fresh sage leaves
- 400g pork fillet
- 1 x 500g block puff pastry
- Plain flour for dusting
- 1 beaten egg

Instructions

1. Heat 1/2 tbsp oil over low heat in a lidded frying pan. Add the onion, cover, and simmer until softened, for 8 mins. Stir in the garlic and simmer for 2 mins, uncovered. Tip into a large bowl and cool absolutely to put aside. When the sausagemeat, breadcrumbs, dried fruit, pistachios, and sage are cooled, add the seasoning. To blend, balance well. Chill and cover.
2. Over a high fire, heat a nonstick frying pan. Rub the pork with 1/2 tbsp of oil, then sear for 2-3 minutes in the pan, turning every 20 seconds until browned all over. To cool absolutely, transfer to a tray.
3. On a sheet of baking paper, put the stuffing. Shape 20cm wide into a rectangle and as long as the pork. Place the pork on top of it and fold it up to enclose the stuffing. Use the paper to help you; use your hands to make the stuffing around the beef. For 30 mins, relax.
4. Meanwhile, roll out one-third of the pastry to a rectangle of around 32 x 18cm on a thinly floured surface. Transfer to a sheet of paper for nonstick baking. Roll the remaining pastry out into a rectangle of 25 x 35cm; transfer to the second sheet of baking paper. For 15 mins, chill both.

5. To a large baking tray, transfer the smaller sheet of pastry. Place the stuffing log in the middle lengthwise and smooth the egg border with the pie. Lift on top of the larger sheet of pastry, then force together with the edges around the beef, softly closing and ensuring that there are no air pockets; trim, leaving around 2-3 cm of pastry. For decoration, reserve any offcuts. Pinch the border of the pie and curl it, then brush it with an egg.
6. If you wish, reroll the trimmings and cut out the festive forms. On top, protect and glaze with the egg. At either point, pierce the pastry and cut a steam hole on top. For 30 mins or up to 6 hours, cover and relax.
7. Heat the oven to 6, 200 ° C, 180 ° C fan steam. Bake the Wellington for 1 hour before the beef is cooked through and crisp. 10-15 mins to recover, then slice to serve.

19. LEEK RAREBIT PORK STEAKS RECIPE

Prep Time: 05 mins

CookTime: 25 mins

Serves: 04

Ingredients

-
- 3 large leeks, washed, trimmed & finely sliced
- 1 tbsp plain flour
- 2 tbsp olive oil
- 125ml dry cider
- 125g grated mature Cheddar
- 1 tsp English mustard
- 4 pork loin steaks, from a 540g pack

Instructions

1. Heat 1 tbsp. of oil in the oven and stir the leeks over medium heat for ten minutes, until they are soft. Set half the leeks in a dish and the other leeks away, cook for 2 minutes, then add in the cider slowly, stirring, until stirred.
2. Add the mustard and cheese and cook slowly, stirring, until it is melted. At this point, the mixture is easy to grab, so be careful.
3. Heat a medium-high barbecue. Heat the rest of oil in a pan over high heat and cook the pork steaks on each side until golden and fried. Cover with a rarebit of leek, then grill until golden for 2-3 mins.
4. Serve with reserved leeks, mashed potato, and broccoli from Tenderstem, if you want.

20. SPICY PORK CHOP TRAYBAKE RECIPE

Prep Time: 15 mins & Serves: 04

Cook + Marinating Time: 30 mins

Ingredients

- 2 red chilies, 1 finely chopped & 1 sliced
- 3 tbsp soy sauce
- 1 tbsp hoisin sauce
- 2 limes, 1 juiced & 1 cut into wedges
- 1.5cm grated piece ginger
- 4 pork chops
- 250g basmati rice, rinsed
- 2 trimmed and sliced leeks
- 1 trimmed and finely chopped lemongrass stalk
- 250g roughly chopped pack pak choi
- 800ml chicken stock
- 15g roughly chopped fresh coriander

Instructions

1. In a non-metallic bowl, mix the finely chopped chili, soy, hoisin, lime juice, and ginger. Add the chops of pork and turn to coat them. Cover and permit to marinate for in any event 30 minutes, or up to 24 hours. 7, 220 ° C, fan 200 ° C. Heat the oven to gas.
2. In a deep roasting pan, blend the rice, leeks, lemongrass, pak choi, and stock. Cover with all the pork and all the marinade, then bake until the pork is fried and the rice is tender for 30 minutes.
3. Garnish with sliced chili and finely minced coriander. Serving to squeeze over with lime wedges.

21. MEDITERRANEAN BONELESS PORK CHOPS WITH JULIENNED VEGETABLES

Prep Time: 15 mins

Cook Time: 20 mins

Total Time: 35 mins

Ingredients

- 16 oz 8 thin sliced centers
- McCormick Montreal Chicken Seasoning, 3/4 tsp
- 1 small, 6 oz zucchini
- 1 small, 6 oz yellow squash
- 1 cup of halved grape tomatoes
- 1 tbsp extra virgin olive oil
- ¼ tsp Kosher salt and fresh cracked pepper
- ¼ tsp oregano
- 3 sliced thin garlic cloves
- Cooking spray:
- 1/4 cup of pitted & sliced Kalamata olives
- 1/4 cup of crumbled Feta cheese
- Fresh juice from 1/2 large lemon
- 1 tsp grated Lemon rind

Instructions

1. Heat oven to 450 degrees. Season the pork chops with seasoning from Montreal.
2. To Julienne the Zucchini and Yellow Squash: Slice the zucchini into 1/8-inch thick slices or use a mandolin fitted with a julienne comb. Cut the slices into 1/8-inch thick strips lengthwise.
3. Add 1/2 tbsp of olive oil, 1/8 tsp of salt, pepper, and oregano to the tomatoes. Place tomatoes cut side up, lightly sprayed with cooking spray on a baking sheet; roast for 10 mins.
4. For another 5 minutes, add sliced garlic and roast (this will prevent the garlic from burning).
5. Cast aside and switch to a large working tub.
6. Lower the oven to 200 ° F.
7. Over medium-high prepare, heat a large nonstick skillet, add 1/2 tbsp of olive oil and zucchini with 1/8 tsp of salt, and sauté until soft, about 5 minutes.
8. Add the tomatoes to the bowl and place them in the warm oven.

9. Spray the cooking spray on the skillet and cook half the pork chops on either side on medium-high heat for around 1 1/2 to 2 minutes, working in two batches. The chops of pork are thin, so you don't want to cook them over, because they're going to be rough. On a platter, set aside.
10. Toss the Kalamata olives, lemon juice, and lemon rind with the vegetables in the oven.
11. Serve the vegetables and finish with Feta cheese over the pork chops.

22. PORK CHOPS WITH PEACHES AND WALNUTS

Prep Time: 02 mins

Cook Time: 15 mins

Servings: 04

Ingredients

- 4 pork chops
- Salt and pepper as need
- 2 tbsp butter
- 1 peach washed and cut into slices
- 1/2 cup of walnuts, chopped in half
- 1 tbsp fresh rosemary leaves
- 2 -3 sprigs of thyme
- 2 tbsp brown sugar

Instructions

1. As needed, season the chops with salt and pepper. Reserve. Reserve.
2. Melt some butter in a pan over medium heat. Add the peach slices and cook for around 2 mins, until well browned on both sides. Place it and take it out of the pan on a plate.
3. Cook the chops on both sides until golden brown, about 5 minutes, in the same skillet.
4. Place the chops over the peaches, walnuts, rosemary, and thyme. Using brown sugar to dust. Cover and cook for roughly 3-4 mins.
5. Instantly serve.

1. BAKED SALMON WITH GARLIC AND DIJON

Prep Time: 05 mins

Cook Time: 15 mins

Ingredients

- 1 1/2 pounds salmon filet
- 2 tbsp parsley chopped
- 2 tbsp lemon juice
- 2 tbsp light olive oil
- 3 garlic cloves pressed
- 1/2 tbsp Dijon mustard
- 1/2 tsp salt
- 1/8 tsp black pepper
- 1/2 sliced lemon

Instructions

1. Heat the oven to 450°F. Silpat or foil a rimmed mixing bowl. Slice salmon into 4 placing on lined mixing bowl, skin-side-down.
2. Combine 2 tbsp of parsley, 2-3 pressed garlic cloves, 2 tbsp of oil and 2 tbsp of lemon juice, 1/2 tbsp Dijon, 1/2 tsp of salt and 1/8 tsp of pepper.
3. Spread the marinade over the salmon top and bottom, then top each part with a lemon slice.
4. Bake 12-15 min at 450°F or until baked smoothly. Don't overcooking.

Cook's Note

Air Fryer Salmon: place salmon on the wire basket, spread marinade over the top and fry at 450 F for 6-7 minutes or until cooked through.

Nutrition Facts

Fat 18g, Saturated Fat 3g, Cholesterol 94mg, Sodium 389mg, Potassium 872mg, Carbohydrates 3g, Fiber 1g, Sugar 1g, Protein 34g

2. HONEY GARLIC SALMON

Prep Time: 10 mins

Cook Time: 05 mins

Total Time: 15 mins

Ingredients

- 12 ounces salmon and cut into 2-3 fillet strips
- Salt and black pepper
- 1 pinch cayenne pepper
- 2 tbsp honey
- 1 tbsp warm water
- 1 1/2 tsp apple cider vinegar
- 1 tbsp olive oil
- 3 minced cloves garlic
- ½ sliced into wedges lemon
- 1 tbsp chopped parsley

Instructions

1. Season salmon with salt, black pepper, and cayenne pepper. Set aside.
2. Mix sugar, water, apple cider vinegar, or lemon juice and pinch salt. Stir well to mix.
3. Heat a high-heat oven-safe skillet. Incorporate olive oil. Pan-fry salmon first, skin side down, around 1 minute. Turn salmon and cook 1 min. Turn again, so the skin side is off.
4. Add the garlic, saute until mildly browned. In the skillet, add the honey mixture and lemon wedges, minimize the sauce until moist.
5. Finish by broiling the salmon in the oven for 1 minute or until mildly charred.
6. Cover with parsley and serve promptly.

Cook's Note

Watch the step-by-step video on this page.

Double the sauce with 4 tbsp of honey, 2 tbsp of warm water, and 3 tsp of apple cider vinegar or lemon juice.

3. SPICY SOUTHERN FRIED CATFISH

Prep Time: 10 mins

Cook Time: 20 mins

Servings: 06

Ingredients

- 2 lbs Catfish Nuggets
- 1 Cup of self rising flour
- 1/2 Cup of yellow cornmeal
- 1/2 Cup of hot sauce
- 2 medium-sized eggs
- 2 tsp your favorite cajun seasoning
- 2- 2 1/2 Cup of oil to fry with

Instructions

1. Make sure the fish is pretty good and clean, then set to the side.
2. Put rice, cornmeal, and cajun seasoning in a big tub. Well blend.
3. Beat the two eggs in a separate bowl, add the hot sauce and blend.
4. Next, substitute the fish with the hot sauce & egg mixture.
5. Make sure the fish is covered with the wet mixture, then coat with the flour mixture.
6. If all the fish is wrapped, set it for about 5 minutes so that the cornmeal & flour mixture will stick well.
7. Heat oil from 350-375 F.
8. Once the oil is nice, add the fish carefully into the skillet or deep fryer, but do not overcrowd.
9. Fry the fish until golden brown, detach from the oil and put on a sheet of paper towel.
10. Let sit until eating is cool enough.
11. Serve and enjoy.

4. CAJUN COMPROMISE CATFISH

Prep Time: 10 mins

Cook Time: 15 mins

Additional Time: 45 mins

Servings: 04

Ingredients

- 2 pounds catfish fillets
- 1 Cup of milk
- 1 egg
- ¼ Cup of all-purpose flour
- ¼ Cup of cornmeal
- 2 tsp ground black pepper
- 2 tsp ground mustard
- 2 tbsp Cajun seasoning
- 1 dash pepper sauce
- ¼ Cup of oil for frying

Instructions

1. Soak the bits in milk for at least 30 minutes.
2. Whisk egg and hot pepper sauce in a small bowl. In a separate bowl, season with rice, cornmeal, vinegar, mustard and cajun. Dip pieces of fish into the dry mixture, then the potato, then the dry mixture. Set on a refrigerator tray, chill for about 15 minutes. This makes the batter adhere to the fish.
3. Heat over enough oil to fill a large heavy skillet at medium-high heat. Fry pieces of fish 3-4 minutes a hand, or until golden brown. Based about how much Cajun seasoning you used, some of the breading can get darker than the others.
4. Drain the fish and eat with hot sauce or tartar sauce. Enjoy it!

Nutrition Facts

448 calories: protein 41.2g: carbohydrates 18.4g: fat 22g: cholesterol 158.1mg: sodium 876.7mg.

5. TASTY TUNA BURGERS

Prep Time: 22 mins

Cook Time: 08 mins

Total Time: 30 mins

Servings: 04

Ingredients

- 1 can drained tuna
- 1 egg
- ½ Cup of Italian seasoned bread crumbs
- ⅓ Cup of minced onion
- ¼ Cup of minced celery
- ¼ Cup of minced red bell pepper
- ¼ Cup of mayonnaise
- 2 tbsp chili sauce
- ½ tsp dried dill weed
- ¼ tsp salt
- ⅛ tsp ground black pepper
- 1 dash hot pepper sauce
- 1 dash Worcestershire sauce
- 4 hamburger buns
- 1 sliced tomato

Instructions

1. Combine fish, egg, bread crumbs, cabbage, celery, red bell pepper, mayonnaise, chili sauce, dill, salt, pepper, sweet pepper sauce, Worcestershire sauce. Well, blend. Shape 4 patties. Refrigerate for 30 minutes to allow handling, if needed.
2. Cover a non-stick skillet with spray cooking: fry tuna patties for around 3 to 4 minutes per hand, or until finished. They're delicate, so be careful when turning.
3. Serve on tomato slices and leaves, if needed.

Cook's Note

The initial tuna can was 6 ounces, which has since been lowered to 5 ounces due to vendor update. Bread crumbs, mayonnaise and seasoning can be marginally decreased.

Nutrition Facts

353 calories: protein 16.4g: carbohydrates 36.6g: fat 15.6g: cholesterol 61.3mg: sodium 779mg

---

6. EASY TUNA PATTIES

Prep Time: 10 mins

Cook Time: 10 mins

Serves: 06

Ingredients

- 3 eggs
- 1 tsp lemon juice
- 3 tbsp grated Parmesan cheese
- 3/4 Cup of Italian-seasoned bread crumbs
- 1 tsp old bay seasoning
- 4 5 ounce cans drained albacore tuna
- 1 tsp dijon mustard
- 1/8 Cup of finely diced onion
- 1/4 Cup of finely diced celery
- 1/4 tsp ground black pepper
- 1/4 tsp dill
- 3-4 tbsp vegetable oil

Instructions

1. Beat bowl eggs and lemon juice. Combine Parmesan cheese, bread crumbs, Old Bay, salmon, mustard, cabbage, celery, black pepper and dill. Add egg/lemon blend.
2. Shape tuna mixture into Eight 1-inch-thick patties.
3. If you have time, refrigerate patties for at least an Hr. This will make them remain longer during frying. This isn't, however, a necessary move.
4. Heat vegetable oil over low heat. Fry until golden brown, around 5 minutes per hand.

Nutrition Facts

Calories: 287kcal, Carbohydrates: 11g, Protein: 33g, Fat: 14g, Cholesterol: 143mg, Sodium: 709mg, Potassium: 345mg, Sugar: 1g, Calcium: 88mg, Iron: 2.3mg.

7. COCONUT SHRIMP

Prep Time: 15 mins

Cook Time: 15 mins

Freeze Time: 30 mins

Ingredients

- 1 pound jumbo shrimp peeled and deveined
- *Salt and pepper*
- *1/2 Cup of all-purpose flour*

Batter:

- 1/2 Cup of all-purpose flour
- 1 tsp baking powder
- 1/2 tsp garlic powder
- 1 egg
- 1/2 Cup of beer

Coating:

- 1 Cup of shredded coconut sweetened
- 1 Cup of Panko bread crumbs

Instructions

1. Line a large parchment-paper baking sheet. Set aside.
2. Place a knife about three-quarters of the way into the shrimp at the tip. Cut a slash down the middle back to the tail. Using your fingertip to partially open shrimp flesh. They needn't be flat. Season with salt and pepper.
3. In a shallow bowl, dredge 1/2 cup of flour. In another small tub, mix together when mixed. The batter should be pancake-like. If too thick, add some additional beer or mineral water between each inclusion.
4. Mix the shredded coconut and crumbs in the third bowl.
5. Dredge in flour, dip in batter, coat in breadcrumb or coconut blend. Press coconut on shrimp gently.
6. Place on baker and repeat with remaining shrimp. Arrange shrimp in one sheet, ice until solid.
7. Heat vegetable oil in a good, hot oven or deep skillet.
8. Fry the Frozen shrimp on either side for 2-3 minutes or until golden brown and crispy. Drain on a paper towel-lined pan.
9. Serve sweet chili sauce instantly.

Cook's Note

Frozen shrimp frying means they don't overcook, thus allowing the crumb time to transform into the delicious golden hue. The coating adheres smoother, not breaking apart.

If you don't have time, fry them as soon as you bread them. Just remember the crumb will start to fall apart after a minute of cooking.

Nutrition Facts

Calories: 417kcal | Carbohydrates: 46g | Protein: 30g | Fat: 11g | Cholesterol: 326mg | Sodium: 767mg | Potassium: 345mg | Fiber: 2g | Sugar: 10g | Calcium: 245mg | Iron: 5.3mg.

8. MISO GLAZED HADDOCK

Prep Time: 25 mins

Cook Time: 20 mins

Total Time: 45 mins

Serving: 02

Ingredients

- 2 thawed haddock filets
- 2 tbsp white miso paste
- 1 tbsp brown sugar
- 2 tsp rice vinegar
- 3 tsp water
- 2 medium-sized zucchinis
- 2 tsp sesame oil
- 1 minced garlic clove
- 1 tsp minced ginger
- Salt as need
- Green onion for garnish

Instructions

1. Preparing the Haddock
2. Heat the oven to 425F. Whisk miso, brown sugar, vinegar and water in a small saucepan. Add to a boil and sauté 1-2 minutes or until the brown sugar has melted.
3. Place fish fillets on a parchment paper-lined sheet tray. Salt and pepper season. Brush with miso paste uniformly. Bake 10 minutes in the oven. Turn the fire to broil and roast for about 5 minutes until the surface has blackened. Careful not to smoke.
4. When frying tuna, make noodles. Cut zucchini into spaghetti using the spaghetti comb. If you don't have a spiralizer, cut the zucchini into thin strips.
5. Using a paper towel to squeeze all the moisture. Hot a medium-high-heat skillet. Add oil, garlic, and ginger. Cook 1-2 minutes or softened. Add zucchini noodles and simmer for 2-3 minutes until wilted. Salt and pepper season
6. Serve tuna noodles. Garnish with green onion.

9. GARLIC BUTTER SHRIMP

Prep Time: 05 mins

Cook Time: 05 mins

Serving: 04

Ingredients

- 4 tbsp butter
- 1 pound large shrimp, peeled & deveined
- Salt and pepper as need
- 1 tsp Italian seasoning
- 2-3 tsp minced garlic
- The juice of one lemon
- 1 tbsp chopped parsley

Instructions

1. Place butter in a wide tub, melt over medium heat. Season with salt, pepper, and Italian seasoning.
2. Cook 3-5 minutes, stirring regularly, until pink and opaque.
3. Add garlic and cook another minute.
4. Add lemon juice and parsley and eat.

Nutrition Facts

Calories: 215kcal | Protein: 23g | Fat: 12g | Cholesterol: 315mg | Sodium: 481mg | Pota ssium: 90mg | Calcium: 176mg | Iron: 2.6g.

10. SPICY GARLIC SHRIMP

Prep Time: 05 mins

Cook Time: 05 mins

Serving: 04

Ingredients

- 1 tbsp olive oil
- 1 pound large peeled and deveined shrimp
- 1 tsp minced garlic
- 1/4-1/2 tsp red pepper
- 1 tsp lemon zest
- 1 tbsp lemon juice
- 2 tbsp parsley
- Salt and pepper as need

Instructions

1. Heat oil in a large skillet.
2. Season with salt and pepper.
3. Cook for 3 minutes and opaque.
4. Add garlic, lemon zest,red pepper flakes: cook 1-2 minutes more.
5. Add lemon juice and petroleum.

Nutrition Facts

Calories: 147kcal | Protein: 23g | Fat: 5g | Cholesterol: 285mg | Sodium: 884mg | Potas sium: 101mg | Calcium: 167mg | Iron: 2.5mg.

11. CAJUN SHRIMP AND RICE SKILLET

Prep Time: 10 mins

Cook Time: 20 mins

Servings: 04

Ingredients

- 1 1/3 cups of grain white rice
- 2 2/3 cups of chicken broth
- 1 pound large or jumbo peeled and de-veined
- shrimp
- 4 tbsp melted divided butter
- 1 tsp minced garlic

Cajun seasoning:

- 1 1/2 tsp paprika
- 1 tsp salt
- 1 tsp garlic powder
- 1/2 tsp cracked black pepper
- 1/2 tsp onion powder
- 1/2 tsp dried oregano may sub an Italian herb blend
- 1/2 tsp cayenne pepper
- 1/4 tsp crushed red pepper flakes

Instructions

1. Whisk together all cajun seasoning ingredients. Melt 2 tbsp of butter over medium-high heat. Add garlic, half cajun spice, and rice.
2. Bring chicken broth to a boil, reduce to a simmer and cover. Cook 15 minutes, stirring 1-2 times.
3. When rice is frying, ready the shrimp with the remaining 2 tablespoons melted butter and remaining cajun seasoning. Pour over shrimp and coat.
4. Stir shrimp into the rice, cover and cook for 3-5 minutes until pink and opaque. Garnish with chopped parsley if needed.

Cook's Note

For brown shrimp, saute the shrimp in the pan at the beginning of the recipe, move to a plate and cover to remain warm until the end, add in rice and eat.

12. HONEY GARLIC GLAZED SALMON

Prep Time: 08 mins

Cook Time: 10 mins

Servings: 04

Ingredients

SALMON:

- 4 salmon filets
- 1/2 tsp kosher salt
- 1/2 tsp black pepper
- 1/2 tsp smoked paprika
- 1/4 tsp blackening seasoning

SAUCE:

- 3 tbsp butter
- 2 tsp olive oil
- 6 minced cloves garlic
- 1/2 cup of honey
- 3 tbsp water
- 3 tbsp soy sauce
- 1 tbsp sriracha sauce
- 2 tbsp lemon juice

Instructions

1. Season with salt, vinegar, paprika and blackening spices. Set aside. Adjust oven rack to center place, then preheat broiler.
2. Add butter and oil to a broad skillet over MED-HIGH fire. When butter is melted, add garlic, water, soy sauce, sriracha, honey, and lemon juice and simmer for about 30 seconds before the sauce is heated.
3. Add salmon, skin side down, and cook 3 minutes. When cooking salmon, occasionally baste with pan sauce by spooning it over the salmon top.
4. Broil salmon for 5-6 minutes, basting once in broil with sauce until salmon is caramelized and cooked to the perfect doneness.
5. Garnish with parsley if needed.

Cook's Note

If you like, season salmon as guided, sear in the skillet. Flip over, sear the other side, and remove to a pan. Add sauce ingredients and cook until hot. Add salmon and spoon sauce over salmon.

13. FURIKAKE SALMON BOWLS

Prep Time: 10 mins

Cook Time: 20 mins

Yield: 02

Ingredients

Salmon:

- 1–2 tbsp sesame oil
- Pinch of salt, pepper, and chili flakes
- 8–10 ounces salmon
- 4 ounces shiitake mushrooms, de-stemmed, sliced

Sauce:

- 3 tbsp soy sauce
- 3 tbsp Mirin
- 1 tbsp Furikake
- Bowl Ingredients:
- 2 extra-large handfuls of shredded cabbage
- 1 sliced avocado
- Feel free to add additional roasted veggies
- Garnish: scallions, furikake, cucumber

Instructions

1. If used, set the rice or grain to prepare.
2. Make Sauce: In a small bowl, mix the soy sauce and mirin.
3. If the shredded cabbage is sauteed, see Cook's Note, and do this now, and set it aside.
4. Cook Salmon: In a large skillet, heat sesame oil over medium-high heat. Using a pinch of salt, pepper, and chili flakes and swirl to season the grease.
5. Add the mushrooms and salmon and sear on both sides until golden. Turn the warmth off and permit the container to cool marginally. Spoon the salmon and mushroom sauce over the end, stirring the skillet. Only set aside.
6. Assemble the bowls: Cut between 2 bowls of rice or seeds. Sprinkle the Furikake with it. Arrange the bowl of lettuce, avocado wedges, and some other vegetables. Sprinkle the seared salmon and mushrooms with Furikake and spoon the remaining sauce over the avocado and cabbage.
7. Serve immediately.

14. GRILLED SHRIMP SKEWERS

Prep Time: 05 mins

Cook Time: 10 mins

Marinating Time: 15 mins

Ingredients

- 1 pound peeled and deveined large shrimp
- 1/4 cup of olive oil
- 2 tbsp lemon juice
- 3/4 tsp salt
- 1/4 tsp pepper
- 1 tsp Italian seasoning
- 2 tsp minced garlic
- 1 tbsp chopped parsley
- Lemon wedges for serving

Instructions

1. In a resealable plastic container, place the olive oil, lemon juice, salt, pepper, Italian seasoning, and garlic together. To mix, seal and shake.
2. To the jar, add the shrimp and seal. Toss with the marinade to coat uniformly.
3. For at least 15 mins to 2 hours, marinate. When the acid in the lemon juice continues to steam the shrimp, you do not want to marinate any longer than that.
4. Thread into skewers with the shrimp. Over the medium-high fire, heat a grill or barbecue pan.
5. On the barbecue, place the skewers. Cook for 2-3 mins or until the shrimp is pink and opaque on either side.
6. Directions for Broiler: Heat the broiler. On a sheet pan sprayed with cooking oil, place the shrimp skewers on. Broil on either side for 2-3 mins, or until the shrimp is pink and opaque.
7. Garnish with parsley. Serve with lemon wedges.

Nutrition Facts

Calories: 206kcal | Protein: 23g | Fat: 10g | Cholesterol: 285mg | Sodium: 1317mg | Potassium: 90mg | Vitamin C: 7.6mg | Calcium: 172mg | Iron: 2.7mg

15. SIMPLE BAKED COD WITH TOMATOES

Prep Time: 10 mins

Cook Time: 15 mins

Yield: 04

Ingredients

- 3 tbsp olive oil
- 2 cups of cherry or grape tomatoes
- 1 1/4 lb cod fillets 4-6 pieces
- Salt, pepper, and chili flakes as need
- 1 lemon zest & slices
- 3 rough chopped garlic cloves
- 1/4 cup of basil leaves torn

Instructions

1. Heat the oven to 400.
2. Load the olive oil into a baking dish measuring 9 x 13 inches. Scatter out the cloves of garlic. Add the lemon slices and tomatoes and toss. Scoot to the left of one.
3. Pat the fish dry and put them in the baking dish, and turn to brush each side of the fish with oil using tongs. Spread out the garlic mixture from the tomato and nestle it in the fish. On the sides, onions beneath the lemons. Season it all with salt, pepper, and chili flakes.
4. Bake for 10 minutes. Give the pan a good shake, quaking a little bit with the tomatoes. With lemon zest, disperse. Bake to your enjoyment for another 5 minutes or until the fish is cooked.
5. Add the broken basil leaves when finished, tossing them with tongs with the heated tomatoes so that the basil wilts somewhat. Then garnish a wilted basil leaf with each slice of cod.
6. Instantly serve!

16. MOROCCAN SALMON

Prep Time: 05 mins

Cook Time: 12 mins

Yield: 02

Ingredients

- 2 salmon filets 4- 6 ounces each
- ½ tsp cinnamon
- ½ tsp cumin
- ½ tsp salt
- ¾ tsp sugar
- Pinch cayenne
- 1 tbsp oil for searing
- Garnish- orange zest

Instructions

1. Heat the oven to 350F.
2. Combine the cinnamon, cumin, salt, sugar, and cayenne in a small bowl.
3. Sprinkle both sides of the salmon over it.
4. Heat oil over medium-high heat in an ovenproof skillet. On both sides, sear salmon for 2 minutes on either side, then place them in the warm oven to finish for 5 minutes or to the perfect doneness.
5. Serve with Moroccan Quinoa Salad and garnish with orange zest.

Cook's Note

Coat two slices of tofu with the spice mix and sear like the salmon to keep this vegetarian. Alternatively, you could sear and crisp the fried chickpeas with spices.

17. BAGELS AND LOX

Prep Time: 13 mins

Cook Time: 02 mins

Servings: 01

Ingredients

- 1 sliced fresh bagel
- 4 ounces smoked salmon
- 2 tbsp cream cheese
- Red onion sliced paper-thin
- Tomato sliced thin

Instructions

1. Cut the bagel horizontally into two. Toast bagel slices, as needed, in a toaster or toaster oven.
2. Spread all of the bagel's sliced sides with cream cheese.
3. 1 bagel half over cream cheese, a slice of smoked salmon, red onion, tomato, and capers.
4. Set the remaining half of the bagel, cream cheese side down, filling over.

Nutrition Facts

Calories: 520kcal | Carbohydrates: 57g | Protein: 33g | Fat: 16g | Cholesterol: 57mg | Sodium: 1542mg | Potassium: 344mg | Fiber: 2g | Calcium: 60mg | Iron: 2.4mg

18. EASY SHRIMP COCKTAIL

Prep Time: 10 mins

Cook Time: 03 mins

Ingredients

- 2 quarts water
- 1 quartered lemon
- 1 or 2 bay leaves
- 10 to 15 whole black peppercorns
- 1 tbsp salt, or as need

Instructions

1. Add the lemon, bay leaves, peppercorns, salt, and bring to a boil over high heat. Fill a big pot of water.
2. To encourage the flavors to mature, allow water to boil for 5 to 10 minutes.
3. Add the shrimp to the water and roast, or once cooked, for 2 to 3 minutes. When they've firmed up and just turned yellow, pull the shrimp. Overcooked shrimp is tough, rubbery, and not healthy.
4. To avoid frying, add shrimp to an ice bath and allow it to stay in an ice bath for around 5 minutes or until cooled.
5. Serve instantly with cocktail sauce or refrigerate for up to 24 hours in an airtight container before serving.

19. EASY STEAMED MUSSELS

Prep Time: 10 mins

Cook Time: 10 mins

Ingredients

- 1 1/2 lbs mussels
- 2 tbsp olive oil
- 4 minced cloves garlic
- 1/2 cup of white wine
- 1 diced tomato
- 1 tbsp lemon juice
- Salt as need
- 2 tbsp chopped parsley, Italian parsley preferred

Instructions

1. Scrub and brush the mussels and, by taking them off, remove the beards on the mussels. Drain yourself and set aside.
2. On medium heat, heat a skillet. Add some olive oil. Before adding the mussels, saute the garlic a couple of times. Stir the mussels and throw them. Combine the white wine with the chopped tomatoes. Cover and steam the skillet with its lid for 1 minute or until all of the mussels are open.
3. Add the lemon juice, salt, and parsley. Stir to blend properly. Serve hot.

20. EASY LEMON GARLIC BAKED TILAPIA

Prep Time: 05 mins

Cook Time: 10 mins

Ingredients

- 4 tilapia filets
- 3 tbsp lemon juice
- 2 tbsp butter melted
- 3 cloves garlic crushed
- salt and pepper as need
- 2 tbsp chopped fresh parsley

Instructions

1. Lay tilapia fillets into a 9x13 baking dish that is lightly greased. Heat the oven to 400°C.
2. Whisk the lemon juice, melted butter, and garlic together in a small bowl. Pour the tilapia over. With salt and pepper, season.
3. Bake for 10-12 mins at 400 degrees before the fish quickly flakes with a fork.
4. Serve hot with extra wedges of lemon and garnish with parsley.

21. EASY BUTTERY SKILLET RECIPE

Total Time: 20 min

Prep Time: 05 min

Ingredients

- 1 1/2 Pounds Cod Fillets
- 2 tbsp Butter
- Season Salt as need

Instructions

1. Over semi-low to medium pressure, heat a nonstick pan on the burner. Dry the cod with paper towels and seasonal changes salt the filets on both sides.
2. When the pan gets wet, a
3. dd the butter to the pan.
4. Swirl it to cover the pan until the butter melts. Add the seasoned cod, next. Cook on the first side for 4-7 mins, depending on the thickness of the fillet.

5. When it's cooked halfway through, flip the fish over. On the sides, you'll see the fillet turning white. It would take longer to cook the larger fillets than the smaller ones.
6. Sear on the second side of the cod and cook for 2-5 more minutes. Remove the fish from the heat, then let it rest for a few minutes. Serving and enjoying.

Nutrition Facts:

Calories: 230, Total Fat: 7.4g, Cholesterol: 95.5mg, Sodium: 235.8mg, Carbohydrates: 0g, Fiber 0g, Sugars: 0g, Protein 39.1g

22. BAKED SCALLOPS WITH CHEESE RECIPE

Prep Time: 10 mins

Cook Time: 08 mins

Serves: 02

Ingredients

- 6 half-shelled scallops if using frozen
- 30 grams unsalted butter cubed
- 2 tbsp mayonnaise
- a small pinch of salt as need; omit if using salted butter
- freshly cracked black pepper as need
- 60 grams shredded mozzarella cheese
- Dried parsley flakes garnishing

Instructions

1. Remove the scallop meat from the casing, thoroughly clean the meat and remove any dirty pieces. To clean, discard hot water and clean the eggs, scald the scallop shells in hot water for a few mins. Place the scallop meat back on the shell.
2. In a small bowl, place the cubed butter and microwave it for 40 seconds. To form a smooth paste, use a spoon to stir the butter vigorously. Add the mayonnaise, salt, and pepper; stir well until well mixed.
3. Place the scallops on a foil or oven tray lined with parchment. Bake the scallops in a 200°C (392°F) pre-heated oven for 5 minutes.
4. Using kitchen tongs, collect the scallop broth gathered in the shells in a small bowl carefully. The broth can be used to flavor other foods.
5. Divide and spoon equally between the scallops with the mayonnaise mixture. And shredded cheese on top.

6.   Place the scallops back in the oven and bake for another 8 minutes or until the cheese is melting at the edges and slightly browned. Floor before serving with dried parsley flakes.

23. EASY SHRIMP PAD THAI

Servings: 06

Ingredients

- 8 ounces rice noodles
- 1/4 cup of ketchup
- 1 Tbsp sugar
- 3 tbsp Thai fish sauce
- 1/2 tsp crushed red pepper
- 2 tbsp divided coconut oil
- 3/4 lb. medium shrimp peeled & deveined
- 1/2 lb. diced boneless chicken
- 2 lightly beaten large eggs
- 1 cup of fresh beans sprouts
- 3/4 cup of sliced green onions extra for garnish
- 1 tsp minced garlic
- 2 Tbsp dry roasted peanuts chopped
- Chopped cilantro for garnish

Instructions

1.   Place the noodles in a big bowl. To cover, add hot water; leave to stand for 15 mins or until tender. Uh, drain.
2.   In a small bowl, combine the ketchup, syrup, fish sauce, and pepper.
3.   In a large nonstick skillet or wok, heat 2 tsp of oil over medium-high heat. Add the shrimp & saute for until the shrimp is cooked. Set aside and cut the shrimp.
4.   Do the same for the bits of chicken before they are finished and put aside.
5.   Then heat 4 tsp of oil over medium-high heat in a pan. Add eggs, cook for 30 seconds or until soft-scrambled, continuously stirring. Add the sprouts, green onions, and garlic and simmer for 1 minute.
6.   Add the mixture of noodles and ketchup, chicken, and shrimp, and boil for 3 to 4 minutes or until heated and soft. Serve with sliced peanuts, chopped cilantro, and wedges of lime.

1. STICKY HONEY GARLIC BUTTER SHRIMP

Prep Time: 05 mins

Cook Time: 15 mins

Servings: 04 People

Ingredients

- 1/2 Cup of Honey
- 1/4 Cup of soy sauce
- 3 cloves minced garlic
- 1 Small Lemon Juice from Lemon
- 1 pound large shrimp deveined and peeled
- 2 tbsp butter
- Green onions for garnish

Instructions

1. In a bowl, whisk sugar, soy sauce, garlic and lemon. Connect half of the sauce and marinate for 30 minutes.
2. Add butter in medium-sized skillet. Add shrimp, conserve marinade. Salt and pepper season.
3. Turn medium-high heat. Cook until two minutes each side turns yellow.
4. Add marinade and spillover shrimp. Cook before sauce thicken and coat the shrimp. Orange onion garnish.

Nutrition Facts

Calories304kcal, Carbohydrates 36g, Protein 25g, Fat 7g, Cholesterol 301mg, Sodium 1743mg, Potassium 153mg, Fiber 1g, Sugar 35g, Calcium 174mg, Iron 2.9mg.

2. HONEY GARLIC BUTTER SHRIMP & BROCCOLI

Marinade: 30 mins

Prep Time: 15 mins

Cook Time: 05 mins

Ingredients

- 1/2 Cup of honey
- 1/4 Cup of soy sauce
- 1 tsp fresh grated ginger
- 2 tbsp minced garlic
- 1/4 tsp red pepper flakes
- 1/2 tsp cornstarch
- 1 pound large shrimp, deveined, peeled and tails removed if desired
- 2 tbsp butter
- 2 Cup of chopped broccoli
- 1 tsp olive oil
- Salt and pepper

Instructions

1. Add sugar, soy sauce, ginger, garlic, red pepper and blend until blended.
2. Place the shrimp in the small bowl, add 1/3 sauce. Marinate 30 minutes.
3. Whisk to the allocated marinade and set aside.
4. Heat a skillet or wok on heat, add olive oil and broccoli, salt and pepper and cook for 5-6 minutes until tender. Delete and set aside.
5. Add butter and shrimp to the skillet, discarding some marinade. Cook until two minutes each side turns yellow.
6. Add the reserved sauce and boil. Add broccoli and toss until heated.
7. Serve with rice or pasta.
8. Garnish with green onions.

Cook's Note

I'm leaving shrimp tails. It adds spice and looks prettier, except if you want to remove them.

Nutrition Facts

Calories 370, Total Fat, 9g, Cholesterol 255mg, Sodium 2175mg, Carbohydrates 45g, Fiber 3g, Sugar 36g, Protein 30g.

3. TOMATO BASIL BRUSCHETTA

Prep Time: 31 mins

Cook Time: 09 mins

Ingredients

- 2 pounds ripe tomatoes
- ½ tsp fine sea salt + more as need
- ½ Cup of finely chopped white onion
- ½ Cup of chopped fresh basil
- 2 minced cloves garlic
- 1 baguette (French bread)
- 4 to 5 tbsp extra-virgin divided olive oil
- Thick balsamic vinegar and Maldon flaky sea salt

Instructions

1. Heat the oven to 45F. Line a wide, rimmed baking sheet with paper for quick clean-up if needed. If your sheet is smaller than mine, you will need to make it in two lots.
2. Dice the tomatoes to a medium mixing bowl, leaving the tomato seeds and juice on the cutting board.
3. Take the salt and add the onion, basil and garlic when they are set. Stir to blend and marinate the mixture when working on the bread.
4. Cut the baguette into bits no more extensive than 1/2-inch. Usually, I can fit twenty to twenty-four slices of bread on my broad baking sheet. Brush each slice gently with olive oil.
5. Place the slices on your lined baking sheet in a single layer and bake them on the center rack for 6 to 9 minutes until crisp and nicely golden. Transfer to a serving platter if needed and set aside.
6. When ready to eat, gently remove the extra tomato juice accumulated in the bowl, using your hand as a stopgap. Add the remaining 2 tbsp of gasoline. Season with additional salt if needed. If you don't believe your bruschetta is garlic enough, add another garlic clove.
7. Top each toast with tomato mixture, tap your bowl spoon to release excess juice if desired. Cover a few tbsp of deep balsamic vinegar and sprinkle gently with flaky salt if you have some. Bruschetta delivered promptly.

4. MARINATED CARROTS

Prep Time: 25 mins

Cook Time: 04 Hrs 30 mins

Total Time: 04 Hrs 55 mins

Ingredients

- 6/7 large carrots
- 2/4 garlic cloves I suggest you try the recipe with less garlic the first time
- 1 tbsp dried oregano
- 2 tbsp cumin
- 1 tbsp smoked Spanish paprika hot
- ⅓ cup of apple cider vinegar
- Salt as need
- Extra virgin olive oil

Instructions

1. Carry about half a gallon of saltwater to a boil.
2. Wash and peel vegetables, add to boiling water
3. Boil the carrots until tender—don't overcook! Then drain them in cold water to let them cool.
4. Mix the garlic and spices so you have a paste.
5. Cut carrots into broad, circular slices and place in your bowl.
6. Add the garlic paste to the carrots, add vinegar and water.
7. Cover the carrots and marinate in the fridge for at least 4 Hrs.
8. Sprinkle with a slotted spoon and serve with high-quality olive oil and salt.

Nutrition Facts

Calories: 83.34kcal Carbohydrates: 11.02g, Protein: 1.3g, Fat: 4.07g,
Sodium: 139.46mg, Potassium: 352.37mg, Fiber: 3.37gSugar: 4.56g, Calcium: 62.18mg,
Iron: 1.5mg.

5. CARAMELIZED BROCCOLI WITH GARLIC

Active Time: 15 mins

Cook Time: 20 mins

Yield: 04

Ingredients

- 3 tbsp extra virgin olive oil
- 2 heads of broccoli stem peeled and heads halved lengthwise
- 1/2 Cup of water
- 3 thinly sliced garlic cloves
- Pinch of crushed red pepper
- Salt and freshly ground black pepper
- 2 tbsp fresh lemon juice

Instructions

1. Heat 2 tbsp in a huge, deep skillet. Add broccoli, cut horizontally, cover and simmer over moderate heat until browned for around 8 minutes.
2. Cover and simmer until broccoli is soft and water evaporates for about 7 minutes. Add the remaining 1 tbsp of olive oil, garlic, and crushed red pepper, and fry uncovered until golden brown, about 3 minutes.
3. Season broccoli with salt and black pepper, add lemon juice and eat.

6. ROASTED BROCCOLI WITH PARMESAN

Prep Time: 05 mins

Cook Time: 20 mins

Yield: Serves 3-4 as a Side Dish

Ingredients

- 1 1/2 pounds broccoli
- 3-4 tbsp virgin olive oil
- Juice from half a lemon
- Kosher salt
- 2-3 minced garlic cloves
- Freshly ground black pepper
- 1/4 Cup of grated parmesan cheese

Instructions

1. Heat the oven to 425°F.
2. Olive oil broccoli, lemon juice, salt: toss broccoli with olive oil and lemon juice until finely coated. Sprinkle salt over broccoli.
3. Arrange florets in one layer on a baking sheet: arrange broccoli florets on a baking sheet with some olive oil or parchment paper or foil.
4. Roast at 425°F for 16-20 minutes until cooked through and finely browned. The best browned bits! Don't panic if you see charring.
5. Place the roasted broccoli in the bowl and toss with lots of freshly ground black pepper and brushed parmesan cheese. Be generous with pepper, and broccoli enjoys it!
6. Serve quickly.

7. BROCCOLI CHEESE BAKE

Prep Time: 30 mins

Cook Time: 35 mins

Servings: 10 People

Ingredients

- 1 pound head of broccoli
- 3 1/2 tbsp butter
- 3 tbsp flour
- 1 1/2 tsp salt
- 2 Cup of milk
- 1 3/4 Cup of shredded swiss cheese
- 2 eggs beaten

Instructions

1. Heat the oven to 325°F.
2. Lightly grease a big bakery.
3. Cooking broccoli in boiling water for about 10 mins.
4. Whisk in flour and salt in a big pot over low heat butter until smooth. Slowly add milk and keep whisking until thickened and start heating. Remove the heat.
5. Fold in cheese and broccoli and mix gently until cheese begins to melt slightly, add eggs and combine gently.
6. Pour into a prepared baking dish, bake 30-45 minutes. Rest 5 minutes before serving. Enjoy it!

Nutrition Facts

Calories: 171kcal | Carbohydrates: 7g | Protein: 9g | Fat: 11g | Cholesterol: 65mg | Sodium: 468mg | Potassium: 234mg | Fiber: 1g | Sugar: 3g | Calcium: 232mg | Iron: 0.6mg

8. GARLIC SAUTEED GREEN BEANS

Prep Time: 05 mins

Cook Time: 10 mins

Ingredients

- 1 tbsp olive oil
- 1 pound fresh trimmed green beans
- 4 minced cloves garlic
- ¼ - ½ tsp salt
- ⅛ tsp black pepper
- 1 squeezed wedge of lemon

Instructions

1. Heat oil medium-high in a large saucepan or non-stick frying pan. Add green beans when heated. Cook for 5-10 minutes, repeatedly tossing until the green beans are softened but a little crisp and blackened in some places.
2. If the beans are browning but still too hard, reduce heat to low and cook gently until you achieve the perfect texture.
3. Add garlic and cook 1 minute longer when stirring frequently to cook garlic. Heat and season with salt, pepper and lemon juice. Serve wet.

Cook's Note

Fat-free: to sauté green beans using water or vegetable broth instead of olive oil.

Olive oil: try applying olive oil for another oil such as coconut oil, avocado oil or vegetable oil.

Nutrition Facts

Calories: 71kcal | Carbohydrates: 9g | Protein: 2g | Fat: 4g | Sodium: 443mg | Potassium: 251mg | Fiber: 3g | Sugar: 4g | Calcium: 47mg | Iron: 1mg.

9. ASIAN MARINATED TOFU

Prep Time: 15 mins

Servings: 02

Ingredients

- 5 tbsp rice vinegar
- 3 tbsp light soy sauce
- 2 tbsp dark soy sauce
- 1 1/2 tsp Asian sesame oil
- 1 tsp sugar
- 3/4 tsp chili paste
- 1 1/2 tsp finely chopped fresh garlic
- 1 1/2 tbsp extra virgin olive oil
- 1 pound extra-firm tofu, pressed and dry-fried

Instructions

1. Gather the Ingredients.
2. Whisk together rice vinegar, mild soy sauces, Asian sesame oil, sugar, chili paste, garlic, and olive oil in a small bowl.
3. Cover and refrigerate before cooking and fry tofu if you haven't already.
4. Place the marinade in a big resealable plastic tub. Add tofu dry-fried bits.
5. Cover the bowl or close the container, refrigerate overnight, and occasionally shake to ensure all the bits are sealed.
6. Tofu storm, save tofu marinade for use as a sauce after stir-frying. Thicken with slurry, if needed.
7. Stir-fry, enjoy!

Cook's Note

There are various types of tofu, from silky and mild to firm and extra-firm: the softer tofu's water content is greater than the firmer types, so if you want to marinate and stir-fry tofu, pick extra-firm.

10. ASIAN GARLIC TOFU

Prep & Cook Time: 01 Hr + 10 mins

Servings: 02

Ingredients

- 1 package super firm tofu
- 1/4 Cup of Hoisin sauce
- 2 tbsp soy sauce
- 1 tsp sugar
- 1 tsp freshly grated ginger
- 2 minced cloves garlic
- 1/4 tsp red pepper flakes
- 1 tbsp olive oil
- 1 tsp sesame oil
- Green onions for garnish
- Rice for serving

Instructions

1. Remove from package tofu. Place about 4 towels on a tray. Set tofu and cover with more paper towels. Place a cast-iron pan or something large on top. Let's wait 30 minutes.
2. Stir Hoisin sauce, soy sauce, sugar, ginger, garlic, and red flakes in a medium bowl.
3. Cut tofu into bite-sized pieces. Place in a sauce bowl and coat. Let's wait 30 minutes.
4. Heat olive oil in a medium-high heat cast iron pan. When hot, add tofu. When brilliantly seared, turn over. Continue cooking until seared.
5. Remove from heat with sesame oil.
6. Sprinkle with green onions and rice.

11. CLASSIC STUFFED PEPPERS

Prep Time: 10 mins

Cook Time: 01 Hr 10 mins

Total Time: 01 Hr 20 mins

Ingredients

- 1/2 Cup of uncooked rice
- 2 tbsp extra-virgin olive oil
- 1 chopped medium onion
- 2 tbsp tomato paste
- 3 minced cloves garlic
- 1 pounds ground beef
- 1 can diced tomatoes
- 1 1/2 tsp dried oregano
- Kosher salt
- Freshly ground black pepper
- 6 bell peppers, tops and cores removed
- 1 Cup of shredded Monterey jack
- Freshly chopped parsley

Instructions

1. Heat the oven to 400°F. Prepare rice in a small saucepan on-box instructions. Heat oil in a medium-heat wide skillet. Cook until tender, about 5 minutes. Incorporate tomato paste and garlic, simmer until fragrant, about 1 minute more. Add ground beef and simmer, breaking meat with a wooden spoon for 6 minutes. Drain some fat.
2. Return beef to skillet, stir in fried rice and diced tomatoes. Oregano, salt and pepper season. Let simmer until liquid drops slightly, around 5 minutes.
3. Place peppers cut side-up in 9"x-13" baking dish and drizzle with oil. Mix spoon beef into each pepper and top with Monterey Jack, then cover with foil.
4. Bake until tender, about 35 minutes. Uncover and bake until bubbly, 10 minutes more.
5. Parsley garnish before serving.

12. MEXICAN QUINOA STUFFED PEPPERS

Prep Time: 10 mins

Cook Time: 01 Hr 25 mins

Total Time: 01 Hr 35 mins

Ingredients

- 1 Cup of quinoa or rice
- 2 scant Cup of vegetable stock
- 4 large red or orange bell peppers
- 1/2 Cup of salsa
- 1 tbsp nutritional yeast
- 2 tsp cumin powder
- 1 1/2 tsp chili powder
- 1 1/2 tsp garlic powder
- 1 15 ounces can black beans
- 1 Cup of whole kernel corn

Instructions

1. Add quinoa and vegetable stocks and cook over high heat. Reduce flame, cover and cook until all liquid is drained and quinoa soft – about 20 minutes.
2. Heat the oven to 375F and grate a 913 baking dish or rimmed baking sheet gently.
3. Brush half peppers with neutral, high-heat oil like avocado oil or distilled coconut oil.
4. Mix then sample and change seasonings accordingly, adding salt, pepper or more spices if needed.
5. Generously stuff half peppers with quinoa mix until all peppers are full, then cover with foil.
6. Cover for 30 minutes. Then cut foil, raise heat to 400F and bake for another 15-20 minutes or until brown is soft and slightly golden. Bake 5-10 minutes for softer peppers.
7. Serve with or as preferred toppings. Best when young, while remaining 2-3 days in the refrigerator. Heat in a 350Foven until wet, around 20 minutes.

Nutrition Facts

Calories: 311, Carbohydrates: 59g, Protein: 14.4 g, Fat: 3.4 g, Cholesterol: 0 mg, Sodium: 498 mg, Fiber: 11.5 g, Sugar: 8.2 g.

13. GREEN VEGETABLE AND RICOTTA TART WITH PARMESAN CRUST

Prep Time: 20 mins

Cook Time: 40 mins

Serves: 06

Ingredients

- 375g firm ricotta
- 1 cup of tightly packed rocket leaves
- 3 lightly beaten eggs, + 1 extra
- 2 chopped spring onions
- 50g finely grated parmesan
- 1 bunch asparagus, thinly sliced using mandoline
- 6 zucchini flowers, sliced lengthways
- ½ cup of thawed frozen peas
- 1 tbs extra virgin olive oil
- ½ tbs white balsamic vinegar
- PARMESAN CRUST:
- 2 cups of plain flour
- ½ cup of finely grated parmesan
- 150g diced chilled unsalted butter
- 1 egg

Instructions

1. Place the rice, parmesan, butter, and 1/2 tsp of salt in a food processor for the crust. Blitz before breadcrumbs resembles it.
2. Add the egg and 1 tablespoon of water. Pulse before a ball emerges. Flatten it into a disk, cover it with plastic tape, and cool it for 20 minutes.
3. Heat the oven to 190°C.
4. In the processor, place the ricotta, rocket, eggs, spring onion, and 1/2 cup of parmesan. Hey, season. Blitz for 1 min or before blended.
5. Roll the pastry into a 5 mm-thick circle on a thinly floured table. Place it on a baking tray lined with parchment. Spread the ricotta mix over the pastry, leaving a 6cm border. Egg brush border, fold overfilling. Brush the egg pastry, then sprinkle with the leftover parmesan cheese. 5-10 mins to relax. Bake for 35-40 minutes and cook until the pastry is golden.
6. Mix the asparagus, zucchini flowers, tomatoes, snow pea shoots, oil, and vinegar in a bowl. Disperse over the tart and serve.

14. SPRING VEGETABLE TART

Prep Time; 15 mins

Cook Time: 20 mins

Serves: 04

Ingredients

- 2 sheets butter puff pastry
- 1 egg, lightly beaten
- 1 tub roasted capsicum and pecorino dip
- 6 halved lengthways baby zucchini
- 3-4 yellow squash, thinly sliced with a mandoline
- 1 thinly sliced bunch of asparagus
- 150g goat's cheese
- Extra virgin olive oil, to serve
- Balsamic vinegar glaze, to serve
- Mixed herbs, to serve

Instructions

1. Heat the oven to 200°C. Cover a big baking tray with paper for baking.
2. Place the pastry sheets on the lined tray side by side to make a tart case. Brush egg wash down one sheet's long side, then overlap by 2cm with the other to make a large single sheet measuring around 36cm x 20cm.
3. Fold and pinch all four edges, pressing down to seal, to make a 2cm border. Border brush with egg cleaner. Prick the tart's foundation all over with a forks. Place the pastry in the oven and bake for 20 minutes or until golden. Remove from the oven and coat the pastry base with a dip.
4. In the meantime, place your vegetables in a big bowl. Pour boiling water over the onions, blanch steeply for 1 min, then drain and pat dry with cooking paper.
5. Scatter over tart vegetables and crumble over goat cheese. Drizzle the glaze with oil and vinegar. Serve with spices that are blended with.

15. MINESTRONE WITH QUINOA AND BRUSSELS SPROUTS

Prep Time: 10 mins

Cook Time: 30 mins

Serves: 04

Ingredients

- 2 tbs extra virgin olive oil
- 150g chopped flat pancetta
- 1 leek, washed & thinly sliced
- 1 finely chopped garlic clove
- 1 chopped carrot
- 1 chopped celery stick
- 400g can chopped tomatoes
- 2 Desiree potatoes, peeled and cut
- 400g can drain borlotti beans
- 350g brussels sprouts, quartered lengthways
- Crusty bread to serve

Instructions

1. In a wide frying pan, heat the oil and pancetta over medium high heat. When the pancetta starts to sizzle, cook until the fat has returned for 2-3 mins.
2. Add the leek, garlic, carrot, and celery, and cook until softened for 2-3 mins. Tomatoes, parmesan rind, potatoes, and 1 liter of water are added.
3. Simmer and then simmer for 15 minutes. Add the beans, sprouts, and quinoa and simmer for an additional 10 minutes until the quinoa is tender and the flavors are infused. Season as needed.
4. Cover with sprouts of blanched Brussels and serve with crusty bread.

16. ONE-TRAY WARM ROAST VEGETABLE SALAD

Prep Time: 15 mins

Cook Time: 02 Hr

Serves: 04

Ingredients

- 3 garlic cloves
- ¼ cup of loosely packed rosemary leaves
- 1/3 cup of olive oil
- ¼ cup of honey
- 1 tsp dried chili flakes, + extra to serve
- 1¼ cup of pecans
- 500g small sweet potatoes, cut into 2cm-thick wedges
- 500g small parsnips, halved lengthways
- 150g thickly sliced semi-soft matured goat's cheese
- 2 cups of loosely packed picked watercress sprigs
- Lemon wedges to serve

Instructions

1. Heat the oven to 180°C. Grease a broad roasting tray with baking parchment and line it.
2. On a chopping board, place the garlic and rosemary together and chop finely. Combine with oil, butter, chili flakes, pecans, and 11/2 tsp salt flakes and transfer to a bowl.
3. Place the prepared tray with the sweet potato, parsnip, and pecan mixture and toss to blend. Spread uniformly around a plate.
4. Using aluminum foil to protect and roast for 1 hour 15 minutes or until vegetables are tender. Remove the foil, lift the oven to 220°C, and roast for 30 minutes or until the vegetables are crispy, turning halfway.
5. Transfer the roast vegetables to a goat's cheese and watercress serving platter. Sprinkle with extra-dried chili and serve with wedges of lemon.

17. LEEK, CHEESE AND MUSHROOM PITHIVIER

Prep & Cook Time: 25 mins + 2 hrs

Serves: 06

Ingredients

- 20g dried porcini mushrooms
- 100g chopped unsalted butter
- 2 thinly sliced leeks
- ½ bunch thyme leaves picked
- 250g sliced Swiss brown mushrooms,
- 2 crushed garlic cloves
- 2 thawed sheets puff pastry
- 1/3 cup of creme fraiche
- 100g coarsely grated gruyere
- 1 lightly beaten egg
- 1 tbs Dijon mustard
- 1/3 cup of olive oil
- 1 witlof, leaves separated
- 1 radicchio, leaves separated
- 1 tbs chardonnay vinegar

Instructions

1. Soak the porcini for 15 mins or until softened in 2/3 cup of boiling water.
2. Warmth half of the spread in an enormous griddle over medium warmth. Add the thyme and leeks. Cook for until the leeks are cozy, mixing them every so often.
3. Add 1/4 cup water, cover, and simmer for 8 minutes or until the leeks are soft but not colored. Reveal and cook for 5 minutes or until there is no fluid. Transfer and set aside in a tub.
4. At high pressure, place the frypan and melt the remaining butter. Add the Swiss brown mushrooms and cook until browned, stirring periodically, for 4-5 mins. Add liquid garlic, porcini, and porcini. Cook for 2-3 minutes or before the liquid disappears. Set to cool aside.
5. Heat the oven to 200 degrees C. Cut a circular of 25cm from 1 sheet of pastry. Spot it on a heating plate fixed with material. Hold the remainder of the sheet cool.
6. Via the cooled leek mixture, stir creme fraiche. Spread half over the round of pastry, leaving a border of 2cm. Cover it with gruyere, then the leek mixture stays.

7. Finish with a mushroom blend that has been cooled. With beaten egg, brush pastry border and top with remaining pastry layer, pushing edges together to seal. To shape a 25cm round, trim the excess pastry and use the back of a knife to score lines from the middle of the pastry to the outer edge. Brush the top of a beaten egg.
8. Bake for 25 minutes or until you have a golden pastry top. Reduce the temperature to 170 ° C and bake for 30 minutes or until crispy on the outside.
9. Spot the mustard and vinegar in a bowl, whisk until mixed, and slowly add the oil. Toss in dressing witlof and radicchio and serve with slices of the warm pithivier.

18. THREE-CHEESE ZUCCHINI GRATIN

Prep Time: 05 mins

Cook Time: 30 mins

Serves: 04

Ingredients

- 6 zucchinis, sliced lengthways
- 2 tbs extra virgin olive oil, + extra to drizzle
- 250g smoked scamorza or dried mozzarella, sliced
- 500g ricotta
- ½ cup of fresh breadcrumbs
- 100g grated pecorino or parmesan
- 50g unsalted butter

Instructions

1. Heat the oven to 180°C. Heat a chargrill pan over high heat.
2. Brush the zucchini with 2 tbs oil. In batches, grill zucchini slices on both sides until charred. Set aside.
3. Grease the base of an ovenproof roasting dish. Place one layer of grilled zucchini, then add some scamorza slices, a few tbsp of ricotta, and a pinch of salt. Repeat the layers until all of the zucchini is used.
4. Sprinkle the top evenly with the breadcrumbs, pecorino, and a pinch of salt. Speck the margarine over the top and dish for 25 minutes or until the top is crunchy and brilliant earthy colored.
5. Serve hot with freshly ground black pepper. Top with micro herbs and drizzle with extra oil.

19. GREEN FRITTATA

Serves: 04

Ingredients

- 1 cup of basil leaves
- 1 cup of flat-leaf parsley leaves
- 2 cups of baby spinach
- 6 eggs
- 500g ricotta
- ¼ cup of parmesan
- 2 tbs extra virgin olive oil, + extra to serve
- 1 sliced onion
- 2 crushed garlic cloves
- 1½ cups of baby kale, + extra leaves to serve
- 1 zucchini, shaved in strips using a vegetable peeler
- 4 stalks of asparagus, shaved into strips with a vegetable peeler
- Lemon juice, to serve

Instructions

1. Heat the oven to 180°C.
2. In a food processor, place the herbs and spinach and whiz until finely chopped. Add the ricotta, eggs, parmesan, and season, then whiz until smooth.
3. Heat oil over low warmth in a griddle. Add the onion and cook for 2-3 mins until softened, then add the garlic and cook until fragrant for another 1 min. Add baby kale and strips of zucchini. Remove yourself from the heat.
4. To blend and spread the Ingredients in the pan, add the egg mixture and stir.
5. Place in the oven and cook until puffed and golden on top, 20-25 mins. Remove from the oven, set aside for 5 mins to cool, then slip out of the pan.
6. Serve with asparagus, extra kale leaves, and drizzle with olive oil and lemon juice.

20. ROASTED VEGETABLE BOWLS WITH GREEN TAHINI

Prep Time: 15 mins

Cook Time: 30 mins

Total Time: 45 mins

Ingredients

Roasted Vegetables:

- 8 peeled and chopped large carrots
- 3 chopped golden potatoes,
- 1 head of broccoli, cut into florets
- 1 head of cauliflower, cut into florets
- Olive oil and salt

Green Tahini:

- 1/2 cup of olive oil
- 1/2 cup of water
- 1/4 cup of tahini
- a big bunch of cilantro and parsley
- 1 clove garlic
- a squeeze of half a lemon
- 1/2 tsp salt

Instructions

1. Heat the oven to 425 degrees.
2. Roasted Vegetables: On a few baking sheets lined with parchment, arrange the vegetables. Toss it with salt and olive oil. For 25-30 mins, roast.
3. Sauce: Blitz the sauce in the food processor or blender while the vegetables are roasting.
4. Finish: Voila! Portion for the week and save! Serve with avocado or hard-boiled eggs or something else that will make life amazing for your lunch.

21. BUTTER PARMESAN CORN

Total Time: 30 mins

Servings: 06

Ingredients

- 6 half ears corn, cleaned, husked
- 2 tbsp butter, softened
- ½ cup of parmesan cheese, grated
- Salt, as need
- Pepper, as need

Instructions

1. Heat the oven to 375ºF.
2. Coat each ear of maize with a thin layer of butter and roll up to coat with the parmesan cheese.
3. In a square baking dish, place the corn and sprinkle it with salt and pepper.
4. Bake for 25 minutes, then.

22. CHEESY GARLIC BROCCOLI

Total Time: 30 mins

Servings: 06

Ingredients

- 3 crowns broccoli
- 1 ¾ cups of shredded cheddar cheese
- 3 crushed cloves garlic
- Salt, as need
- Pepper, as need

Instructions

1. Heat the oven to 375ºF.
2. In a medium rectangular casserole bowl, layout the broccoli.
3. In a separate bowl, stir the garlic and cheddar cheese together.
4. Sprinkle the cheese over the broccoli equally and add salt and pepper if necessary.
5. 25 mins to bake.
6. Enjoy

1. TRADITIONAL IRISH SODA BREAD

Prep Time: 15 mins

Cook Time: 45 mins

Total Time: 01 Hr

Ingredients

- 1 3/4 cups of all-purpose flour
- 1 3/4 cups of wheat flour
- 1 tsp salt
- 1 tsp baking soda
- 2 tbsp cold butter
- 1 egg
- 1 ⅔ Cup of buttermilk
- 1 tbsp oats

Instructions

1. Heat the oven to 425°F.
2. Mix flours, salt and soda in a large pan. Add butter and rub with your finger Cook's Note into the flour mix until it resembles crumbs.
3. Whisk egg and buttermilk in a different jug.
4. Make a well in the middle of dry ingredients and pour in the flour mixture 3/4 at once.
5. Using an open side, mix flour and liquid into a loose dough. Dough should be smooth, but not sticky. You'll know if it wants more liquids.
6. Turn onto a floured work surface and carefully place the dough together about 1 1/2 inches thick.
7. Place well-dusted flour on a baking sheet
8. Score the deep-cross bread on top. Poke a hole in the bread's 4 corners to free the fairies and avoid them cursing your precious bread.
9. Glaze the bread with the remaining buttermilk and sprinkle the top with dried oats.
10. Bake for 15 minutes, turn the oven to 400°F, and bake for 30 minutes. The loaf can sound mildly hollow when tapped down. Remove from the sheet to cool on a shelf.

Cook's Note

For each Buttermilk Cup, mix 1 Cup of normal milk with 2 tbsp of lemon juice or white vinegar. Mix and let stand 30 minutes before using.

2. YOGURT FLATBREADS

Prep Time: 20 mins

Cook Time: 10 mins

Servings: 08

Ingredients

- 1 ½ Cup of or more unbleached all-purpose flour
- 2 ½ tsp. herbs de Provence or any herbs – basil, oregano, thyme
- 1 ½ tsp baking powder
- ½ tsp baking soda & ¾ tsp salt
- ¾ Cup of low fat or non fat plain greek yogurt
- 2 Tbsp canola oil plus extra for oiling the griddle

Instructions

1. In a large bowl, add seasoning, baking powder, salt and soda. Shake to mix. Add yogurt and 2 tbsp of oil and blend until all flour is combined.
2. Dust a flour cutting board and pour the mixture. Knead the dough until smooth, not sticky, adding some flour if necessary. Divide dough into 8 bits and roll cubes.
3. Using a pin, roll each ball to 1/4 inch thick.
4. Heat a grid over medium heat and spray with canola oil. When the pan is hot, add the dough and cook, turn after 3-4 minutes or when the bottom is orange. Cook 3-4 minutes until golden brown. Serve warm with butter or rubbed with olive oil.

Cook's Note

I made these with all-purpose and whole wheat flour. When using whole wheat flour, you will need to add a little more yogurt if it is too dry. I used dried herbs in these, but use fresh herbs – begin with 2 Tbsp. See if you like taste. As for herbs, you can use any herbs/spices you want and compliment whatever you serve them!

Nutrition Facts

Calories: 134kcal | Carbohydrates: 19g | Protein: 4g | Fat: 4g | Sodium: 295mg | Potassium: 139mg | Fiber: 1g | Calcium: 86mg | Iron: 3.1mg.

3. GREEK YOGURT BANANA BREAD

Prep & Cook Time: 15 mins & 01 hr

Servings: 08

Ingredients

- 2 Cup of all-purpose flour
- 1/4 Cup of light brown sugar
- 1/2 Cup of sugar
- 1/2 tsp salt
- 1 tsp baking soda
- 3 very ripe, mashed well, darkly speckled bananas
- 1/4 Cup of plain greek yogurt
- 2 large eggs
- 1/4 Cup of vegetable oil
- 2 1/2 tsp vanilla extract
- 1 Cup of chopped walnuts or chocolate chips

Instructions

1. Heat the oven to 350°F. Cover a 9-inch loaf pan with parchment paper, then coat the parchment paper.
2. Flour, sugar, brown sugar, baking soda and salt in a large bowl.
3. Mashed bananas, eggs, Greek yogurt, olive oil and vanilla extract in a separate medium bowl. Connect the wet ingredients to the dry ingredients and stir. Add sliced nuts or chocolate chips and scrape the batter into the prepared pan.
4. Bake 50-60 minutes until the inserted toothpick is clean.
5. Take the bread from the oven and allow it to cool entirely in the saucepan before using the parchment paper overhangs.

4. STRAWBERRY YOGURT BREAD

Prep Time: 10 mins

Cook Time: 45 mins

Ingredients

- 1/ 3 Cup of melted butter
- 1 Cup of sugar
- 2 eggs
- 1 tsp zest lemon
- 1 1/ 2 Cup of all-purpose flour
- 1 tsp baking powder
- 1/ 2 tsp salt
- 1/ 2 Cup of plain greek yogurt
- 1 1/ 2 Cup of fresh strawberries

Instructions

1. Heat the oven to 350ºF.
2. Prepare a loaf, oil it and set aside.
3. Melt butter, sugar, eggs and lemon juice in a medium bowl.
4. Meal, salt and powder in another bowl. Mix wet and dry products slowly. Add Greek yogurt and stir until finely mixed.
5. Dice half the sum of strawberries with the lemon zest. Cut the remaining strawberries and set aside.
6. Pour into your greased loaf pan and top the strawberry halves in one sheet. Bake 45-50 minutes or until a toothpick is clean.
7. Cool to room temperature. Cut and serve.

5. YOGURT CHOCOLATE CHIP BREAD

Prep & Cook Time: 15 mins + 30 mins

Servings: 12

Ingredients

- 2 Cup of cake flour
- 1 1/2 tsp baking powder
- 1/4 tsp baking soda
- 1 pinch salt
- 1/2 Cup of semi sweet mini chocolate chips
- 1/4 Cup of ground walnuts
- 1/2 Cup of vegetable oil
- 1 Cup of sugar
- 3/4 Cup of Greek yogurt
- 1 tbsp milk
- 2 eggs
- 1 egg yolk

Instructions

1. Heat the oven to 340°F. Lightly oil, starch 8 1/2 inch.
2. Meal, baking powder, baking soda, flour, chocolate chips and nuts in a large bowl.
3. In a wide bowl with a whisk, mix oil, sugar, cream, milk, eggs and yolk.
4. Fold with a spatula in the flour mixture until all the flour has been mixed.
5. Add the prepared loaf/cake pan and bake for around 30-35 minutes, check for toothpick doneness, let cool for 5 minutes, and remove powdered sugar to a wire rack if necessary. Enjoy it!

Nutrition Facts

Calories: 315kcal | Carbohydrates: 38g | Protein: 6g | Fat: 16g
| Cholesterol: 45mg | Sodium: 44mg | Potassium: 166mg | Fiber: 1g | Sugar: 21g | Calcium: 54mg | Iron: 1mg.

6. STRAWBERRY BREAD

Prep Time: 30 mins

Cook Time: 45 mins

Additional Time:10 mins

Servings: 24

Ingredients

- 2 Cup of fresh strawberries
- 3 ⅛ Cup of all-purpose flour
- 2 Cup of white sugar
- 1 tbsp ground cinnamon
- 1 tsp salt
- 1 tsp baking soda
- 1 ¼ Cup of vegetable oil
- 4 beaten eggs
- 1 ¼ Cup of chopped pecans

Instructions

1. Heat the oven to 350F. Butter and two 9 x 5-inch loaf sheets.
2. Slice strawberries in a medium-sized bowl. Sprinkle with sugar and set aside before preparing batter.
3. Combine sugar, butter, cinnamon, salt and baking soda in large bowl. Pour oil and eggs into strawberries. Add strawberry mixture to flour mixture before dry ingredients are moistened. Drop pecans. Cut batter into pans.
4. Bake in a preheated oven until a center tester is clean, 45 to 50 minutes. Cool on wire rack for 10 minutes. Turn loaves and allow to cool before slicing.

Nutrition Facts

Per Serving: 281 calories: protein 3.3g: carbohydrates 31.2g: fat 16.6g: cholesterol 31mg: sodium 161.5mg.

7. GLAZED STRAWBERRY BREAD

Prep Time: 15 mins

Cook Time: 55 mins

Total Time: 01 Hr 10 mins

Ingredients

Bread:

- 2 Cup of all-purpose flour
- 1 tsp baking soda
- 1/2 tsp salt
- 1/4 tsp ground cinnamon
- 1 large room temperature egg
- 3/4 Cup of granulated sugar
- 1/4 Cup of packed light
- 1 Cup of buttermilk
- 1/3 Cup of vegetable oil
- 2 tsp pure vanilla extract
- 1 and 1/2 Cup of fresh strawberries, rinsed, dried, chopped

Glaze:

- 1 Cup of confectioners sugar
- 1/2 tsp pure vanilla extract
- 2 tbsp heavy cream

Instructions

1. Heat the oven to 350°F. Spray a 9×5 loaf spray pan. I prefer a dark metal loaf pan, which seems to support quicker brown breads.
2. Make bread: toss the flour, baking soda, salt, and cinnamon in a wide bowl until mixed. Set aside. Whisk egg, granulated sugar and brown sugar in a medium bowl until mixed. Assure no residual brown sugar lumps. Whisk buttermilk, oil, cocoa. Mix wet ingredients and stir until there are no lumps. Try hard not to overmix, resulting in a rough-textured bread. Fold strawberries.
3. Bake the bread for 50-1 Hrs. After 30 minutes, I cover the bread loosely with aluminum foil to avoid it being too brown. Poke the bread core with a 50-minute toothpick. If it's safe, the bread's finished. If it's wet, bake longer. Oven times differ between ovens. My bread took precisely 58 minutes. Enable bread to cool completely before glazing and slicing on a wire rack.

4. Make the glaze: Mix sugar, vanilla, and cream together until mixed and smooth. Remove bread directly before serving. Bread remains fresh at room temperature for up to 1 week. Day 2 intensifies bread's taste and moisture!

8. STRAWBERRY BANANA BREAD

Prep Cook Time: 15 mins + 30 mins

Servings: 12 Slices

Ingredients

- 1/2 Cup of butter softened
- 1 Cup of granulated sugar
- 2 large eggs beaten
- 3 ripe bananas mashed
- 2 Cup of flour
- 1 tsp baking soda
- 1/2 tsp salt
- 1 1/2 Cup of fresh strawberries chopped & tossed in 1 tbsp of flour

Instructions

1. Heat the oven to 375F. Spray two nonstick-spray 9x5 loaf pan. Set aside.
2. Use a KitchenAid Stand Mixer of cream butter and sugar in a large bowl until smooth and fluffy.
3. In a bowl, beat forked eggs. Add eggs, beat until mixed. Attach bananas as combined.
4. Ingredients: rice, baking soda, salt. Add sealed dry ingredients to the banana mixture and blend until flour is mixed.
5. Combination! Fold in wrapped strawberries.
6. Pour flour into prepared loaf pans, bake 15 minutes at 375F. REDUce heat to 350F and bake until the sides are slightly brown or until the toothpick inserted into the middle comes out clean. Let cool before removing from loaf pans.

Nutrition Facts

Calories254kcal, Carbohydrates41g, Protein4g, Fat9g, Cholesterol55mg, Sodium270mg, Potassium168mg, Fiber2g, Sugar21g, Calcium15mg, Iron1mg.

9. BUTTERMILK CORNBEAD

Prep Time: 15 mins

Cook Time: 30 mins

Ingredients

- 1 1/2 Cup of cornmeal
- 1 Cup of all-purpose flour
- 1/3 Cup of sugar
- 4 tsp baking powder
- 1 tsp kosher salt
- 2 Cup of reduced-fat buttermilk
- 1 large egg
- 6 tbsp melted and divided unsalted butter

Instructions

1. Heat the oven to 425F. Place a 10-inch cast-iron skillet, oven-proof.
2. Combine cornmeal, rice, sugar, baking powder, salt in a large bowl.
3. Whisk buttermilk, egg and 3 tablespoons butter in a large glass mixing cup or bowl. Pour over dry ingredients and rubber spatula until moist.
4. Remove the skillet from the oven until hot, around 1-2 minutes.
5. Scoop right into the skillet. Bake 25-30 minutes or until clean. Cool 5 minutes.
6. Serve warmly.

10. CHEESE GARLIC BREAD

Prep Time: 09 mins

Cook Time: 06 mins

Ingredients

- 4/5 slices of bread or half a loaf of bread
- 2 tbsp salted or unsalted butter
- 3 to 4 medium minced garlic
- ½ Cup of grated cheese, processed or cheddar
- Salt as required to be added
- Red chili flakes as required
- Dry oregano or any herb as required
- Black pepper as required

Instructions

1. Heat the oven for 392F before starting.
2. Slice the bread loaf into 0.75-inch slices. Half each slice.
3. Take 2 tbsp of soft butter. I used butter salted. If using unsalted butter, add salt.
4. Grate 3 to 4 medium garlic directly into butter. You should also incorporate garlic chives instead.
5. Mix the rubbed garlic with honey.
6. 100 grams cheddar or mozzarella cheese. Around 1/2 Cup rubbed cheese.

Making Cheese Garlic Bread:

1. Spread the garlic butter on both slices equally.
2. Cover the cheese generously.
3. Sprinkle with your favorite spice. Oregano, garlic, red chili flakes, black pepper, Italian seasoning etc.
4. Place the slices in a baking tray.

Baking Garlic Cheese Bread:

1. Now keep the baking tray on your otg's topmost shelf. If using a convection microwave oven, keep the baking tray on the glass turntable.
2. Bake at 392 degrees Fahrenheit for 5 to 6 minutes before the sides turn golden and slightly crisp.
3. The cheese also melts. You needn't toast these slices.
4. Serve them hot with tomato ketchup as a starter or as a snack.

Cook's Note

- To make garlic on a stovetop or tawa
- Heat thick tawa on a medium flame.
- Keep the flame lowest, place the bread slices on the tawa.
- Cover so that the cap doesn't hit the grated cheese.
- Roast before cheese melts for a few minutes.

11. FRENCH BREAD ROLLS

Prep Time: 02 Hrs

Cook Time: 20 mins

Total Time: 02 Hrs 20 mins

Ingredients

- 1 1/2 Cup of warm water
- 1 tbsp yeast
- 1 tbsp sugar
- 2 tbsp olive oil
- 1 tsp salt
- 4 Cup of flour

Instructions

1. In a wide bowl, add yeast and sugar, and sit for about ten minutes.
2. Connect oil, salt, and 2 cups of meal to the yeast mixture. Mix well.
3. Add another 1 1/2 cup flour mixture and blend properly. Using dough hook while using a stand mixer.
4. Add another 1/2 cup flour until smooth and elastic. Cover and let rise until doubled, about 30-60 minutes.
5. Punch and transform on floured board. Divide the dough into 16 equal parts.
6. Place the two inches apart balls on lightly greased baking sheets. Cover with a cloth and lift until multiplied. Preheat oven to 400F. As rolls rise.
7. Bake 400F. 18-20 minutes, golden brown.

12. BANANA BREAD ROLLS

Chill Time: 02 Hrs

Cook Time: 12 mins

Service: 08

Ingredients

- 3/4 Cup of all-purpose flour
- 1 tsp baking powder
- 1/2 tsp salt
- 3 eggs
- 3/4 Cup of granulated sugar
- 1 1/2 Cup of mashed bananas
- 1 1/2 tsp divided vanilla extract
- 1 Cup of confectioner's sugar + extra for sprinkling
- 1 package softened cream cheese
- 1/4 Cup of softened butter
- Chocolate sauce for drizzling
- 1/4 Cup of chopped walnuts

Instructions

1. Heat the oven to 375F. Cover a 10-x-15-inch rimmed baking sheet with spray.
2. Combine flour, baking powder, and salt in a medium bowl: combine well.
3. In a wide tub, with a high-speed electric mixer, beat eggs for 4-5 minutes or until fluffy. Beat rice, bananas, 1 tsp vanilla. Fold the banana mixture until mixed.

4. Bake 12-15 minutes or until clean. Remove from the oven and invert to a clean kitchen towel coated with pastry powder. Although cake is still hot, roll it up from the narrow end: cool on a wire rack. Unroll cake when cold, remove towel.
5. Beat 1 cup of confectioner's sugar, cream cheese, butter, and remaining vanilla in a small bowl at medium tempo. Spread over cake, fold it up again. Chill for least two Hrs. Sprinkle with chocolate syrup and nuts until ready to eat, and cut into 1/2-inch slices.

Cook's Note

If you can't get enough tasty banana recipes, review our Irresistible Banana Recipes list.!

13. SWEET POTATO CHALLAH

Makes: 02 Braided Loaves

Ingredients

- 1 1/4 cups of warm water
- 1 tbsp active dry yeast
- 1/2 cup of honey
- 2 tbsp melted butter
- 1 whole egg + 2 yolks
- 2 tsp salt
- 4-6 cups of unbleached all-purpose flour
- 1 cup of cooked, mashed sweet potatoes
- Egg wash

Instructions

1. In a bowl, disintegrate the yeast in warm water. Mix the sugar, butter, yolks, eggs, mashed sweet potatoes, and salt. Add some flour in turn, beat with every option, consistently plying with your hands as the mixture thickens.
2. Work until smooth and versatile and not tacky any longer, adding flour if necessary. Cover with a clean, moist cloth and let rise for 1 1/2 hours or until the bulk of the dough has doubled.
3. Punch the risen dough down and move to a floured surface. Divide in half and knead each half for five minutes or so, adding flour to avoid stickiness if needed. Shape dough into forms that are desired. I shaped mine into 6 braids of strands.
4. Grease two baking trays and put each one with a finished braid or round. Cover with a towel and quit to stand for an hour or two. Heat the oven to 350°F. With 1 tbsp of water, beat one egg and spray a generous amount over each braid.
5. Bake for approximately 25 mins at 350 degrees F. Cool for at least one hour on a rack before cutting.

14. PARKER HOUSE ROLLS

Makes: 36 Servings

Ingredients

- 1 envelope active dry yeast
- 1 cup of whole milk
- ¼ cup of vegetable shortening
- 3 tbsp sugar
- 1½ tsp kosher salt
- 1 large egg, room temperature
- 3½ cups of all-purpose flour, + more for surface
- Canola oil (for the bowl)
- ¼ cup of unsalted butter
- Flaky sea salt

Instructions

1. In a bowl, whisk the yeast and 1/4 cup of warm water; let stand for 5 mins.
2. Heat the milk until wet in a small saucepan over medium heat. In a wide bowl, combine the shortenings, sugar, and kosher salt. Add warm milk; whisk to mix, shortening it to small clumps. Whisk in the egg and yeast combination.
3. Add 31/2 cups of flour; stir vigorously until the dough shapes with a wooden spoon. Knead the dough until soft, 4-5 minutes on a lightly floured surface, with lightly floured palms.
4. Transfer to a bowl that is lightly oiled; turn to coat. In the plastic tape, cover loosely. Let stand at room temperature, around 11/2 hours, until doubled.

5. Gas the furnace to 350°. In a small saucepan, heat the butter. Brush the baking dish gently with some molten butter. Punch the dough down; cut it into four equal parts. "Roll out into a 12x6" rectangle on a gently floured board, dealing with 1 piece at a time.
6. Cut into three 2-inch-wide strips lengthwise; cut into three 4x2-inch rectangles each crosswise.Brush half of each with the melted butter; fold over the unbuttered side, allowing a 1/4-inch overhang. Place flat against the short side of the dish in 1 corner of the dish, folded edge against the short side of the dish.
7. Add remaining rolls, shingling to shape 1 long row. Repeat for 4 rows of the remaining dough. Brush with melted butter, plastic loosely coated,
8. 25-35 mins, bake rolls until golden and puffed. Brush with butter; scatter over sea salt. Serve warm.

15. LEMON RASPBERRY LOAF

Prep & Cook Time: 10 mins + 01 hour

Yield: 06 Servings

Ingredients

- 1 ½ cups of flour
- 1 ½ tbsp of baking powder
- 1 cup of buttermilk
- 2/3 cup of sugar
- 3 eggs
- 1/3 cup of vegetable oil
- 1 ½ cups of fresh raspberries
- Zest of ½ lemon

For the glaze:

- 1 cup of powdered sugar
- ¼ cup of lemon juice

Instructions

1. Heat the oven to 350 F.
2. Whisk in the flour and baking powder. Whisk together the eggs, buttermilk, palm oil, and sugar in another bowl.
3. Mix the dry components with the wet components and whisk until well mixed. Add framboise.
4. Pour the batter into an 8.5 to 4.5 to 2.5 inch greased loaf pan and bake for until the toothpick is clean. Enable it to cool absolutely.
5. Whisk up the glaze Ingredients.
6. Pour the glaze over the loaf and add lemon zest to the end.

16. PUMPKIN BANANA CHOCOLATE CHIP BREAD

Servings: 2 Loaves

Ingredients

- 3/4 cup of unsalted butter softened
- 3 eggs
- 1 cup of canned pumpkin
- Light brown sugar, 1 1/2 cups
- 2 bananas extra ripe
- 3 cups of flour
- 2 tsp baking soda
- 1 1/2 tsp pumpkin pie spice
- 1/2 tsp baking powder
- 1/2 tsp salt
- 1 cup of semi-sweet chocolate chips

Instructions

1. Heat the oven to 350 degrees.
2. Combine the brown sugar, butter, and eggs in a large bowl. Mix for roughly 1 to 2 mins until light and fluffy.
3. Add the bananas and pumpkin. Blend fine, 1 to 2 minutes.
4. Add the majority of the ingredients, except for the chocolate chips. Mix until it is just moistened, around 1 min.
5. Stir the chocolate chips together.
6. In 2 greased loaf pans, pour in.
7. Bake for a time of 40 to 50 mins.
8. Cool and remove from the pans for five mins.

17. CINNAMON SWIRL BREAD RECIPE

Cook Time: 60-70 mins

Cooling Time: 10 mins

Ingredients

Bread Mix:

- 2 cups of flour
- 1 cup of sugar
- 2 cups of flour
- 1 cup of sugar
- 1 tsp baking soda
- 1/2 tsp salt
- 1 cup of buttermilk
- 1 egg
- 1/4 cup of vegetable oil

Cinnamon Swirl:

- 1/2 cup of sugar
- 3 tsp cinnamon

Glaze:

- 1/4 cup of powdered sugar
- 2 tsp milk

Instructions

1. Heat the oven to 350 degreesF.
2. In a bowl, mix the flour, 1 cup of sugar, baking soda, and salt.
3. Mix the buttermilk, egg, and oil in a separate dish. Stir in the combination of flour when saturated.
4. Mix the cinnamon and 1/2 cup of sugar in a small bowl.
5. Use cooking spray to spray the bottom of a loaf pan.
6. Sprinkle 2/3 of the mixture with the cinnamon swirl, then return half the batter to the tray.
7. Sprinkle the leftover batter with the remaining cinnamon swirl mixture.
8. Take a spatula or knife and chop it into the batter to churn.
9. Bake for 60-70 mins, or until the inserted toothpick comes out clean.
10. In the pan, cool for 10 minutes, then slice and place the bread loaf on the cutting board.

11. Place the powdered sugar in a bowl and add the milk slowly, stirring until you reach the consistency of the syrup. Swirl over a loaf.

18. CARAMEL PECAN SWEET BREAD

Prep Time: 30 mins

Cook Time: 25-40 mins

Ingredients

- 2 cups of Flour
- 2 & 1/2 tsp of Baking Powder
- 3/4 cup of Sugar
- 1 tbsp of Instant Coffee
- 1 tsp of Salt
- 2 lightly beaten Eggs
- 2/3 cup of Milk
- 1/2 a cup of Melted Butter
- 2 tbsp of Butter
- 3/4 cup of Brown Sugar
- 1/2 a cup of Pecans

Instructions

1. Start by adding a large mixing bowl with your flour, baking powder, sugar, coffee, and salt.
2. When well blended, whisk or sift together.
3. Add 2 eggs, milk, and melted butter to the mixture.
4. Mix until well mixed, using a hand mixer or a stand mixer with a dough attachment.
5. Place the dough in a bread loaf pan that's well greased.
6. Mix the butter, brown sugar, egg, milk, and pecans in a big mixing bowl.
7. Mix and spill the dough over it.
8. With a knife, cut into the dough to allow the pecan mixture to saturate.
9. Bake for 25 mins at 350 degrees. If the bread is not baked, transfer to the top rack, minimize it to 200 and bake for another 15 minutes.
10. Serve and enjoy.

Cook's Note

If you like smoother caramel, butter and brown sugar should be creamed together first. Then add the egg and milk, and cook until it becomes thick in a saucepan. Proceed with stages 7 to 10.

19. COCONUT BANANA BREAD

Prep Time: 05 mins

Cook Time: 01 hour

Coconut Flakes: 15 mins

Servings: 10

Ingredients

- 1/2 cup of melted unsalted butter
- 1 cup of white granulated sugar
- 2 eggs room temperature
- 2 cups of all-purpose flour
- 1 tsp baking soda
- 1/4 tsp salt
- 1 tsp vanilla extract
- 3 large ripe bananas
- 1 cup of coconut flakes packed
- Milk enough to cover coconut flakes

Instructions

1. Place a measuring cup of coconut flakes and add enough milk to cover the flakes. Let it settle down for about 10-15 mins.
2. Heat the oven to 350°F. Grease an 8x4 baking dish with bread.
3. Mix the banana with a fork in a big mixing dish.
4. Whisk together the eggs, sugar, melted butter, and vanilla extract.
5. Add the rice, baking soda, and salt and whisk gently until the mixture is thick and finely combined.
6. Squeeze the milk from the coconut flakes and add the batter to the flakes. Fold them inside.
7. Transfer the batter into the baking dish that was packed. 55-60 mins to bake. To hold direct heat away, loosely cover with aluminum foil if the top of the bread is browning too rapidly.
8. Take out the bread, and before cutting, let it cool. Cut the bread with a serrated bread knife.

Cook's Note

Lyubov Brooke All photos and text for. Will Cook For Smiles. Without prior permission, please do not use my photos.

Please link back to this post for the recipe if my articles are included in collections and features. Disclaimer: The dietary details shown are not known to be 100% correct since most products and products differ slightly.

Nutrition Facts

Calories: 351kcal | Carbohydrates: 49g | Protein: 4g | Fat: 15g | Cholesterol: 57mg | Sodium: 201mg | Potassium: 211mg | Fiber: 2g | Sugar: 25g | Calcium: 15mg | Iron: 1.7mg.

20. PALEO DARK CHOCOLATE BROWNIE BREAD

Prep Time: 05 mins

Cook Time: 60 mins

Yield: 8 Slices

Ingredients

- 1/2 cup of liquid coconut oil
- 1 flax egg or 1 pasture-raised egg
- 1 cup of unsweetened almond milk
- 1 tsp vanilla extract
- 3/4 cup of coconut sugar
- 2 1/2 cups of almond flour
- 1/2 cup of cacao powder
- 3 tsp baking powder
- 2 chopped Hu Kitchen Salt Dark Chocolate Bars

Instructions

1. Heat the oven to 350 degrees. Line well with a loaf pan
2. Mix the coconut oil, flax egg, milk, and vanilla extract in a large mixing bowl until well mixed.
3. Incorporate coconut sugar, almond flour, cacao powder, and baking powder when mixed uniformly.
4. Fold in half the dark chocolate and blend well.

5. Add the flour to the loaf pan and bake in the oven for 20 minutes, then cover with the leftover chocolate, sprinkle with chocolate, and cook for another 45-55 minutes.
6. Let the loaf cool for 10 mins, then slice it and eat it.

Cook's Note

Place leftovers in airtight containers on the fridge for up to 5 days or freeze for a few months.

21. CINNAMON ROLL BREAD

Prep Time: 10 mins

Cook Time: 50 mins

Ingredients

- 1 cup of sugar
- 2 cups of flour
- 1 Tbsp baking powder
- 1/2 tsp salt
- 1 egg
- 1 cup of milk
- 1/3 cup of vegetable oil

SWIRL IN:

- 2 tsp cinnamon
- 1/3 cup of sugar

TOPPING:

- 4 tbsp butter softened
- 2 cups of powdered sugar
- 1 tsp vanilla
- 3 tbsp milk

Instructions

1. Heat the oven to 350 degrees. 1.5 Poon Loaf Pan Oil.
2. Add the baking powder, sugar, flour, and salt together in a medium mixing bowl.
3. Whisk in the eggs, milk, and oil until they're all damp.
4. Combine the cinnamon and sugar in a flavorful sauce.

5. In a loaf pan, pour half the bread batter. Place half the mixture of cinnamon-sugar on top. When using a knife or a spatula, churn.
6. Use a knife or spatula to dump the remaining mixture on top, top with the remaining cinnamon sugar, and swirl.
7. Bake in the middle for 1 hour or until a toothpick comes out clean. Enable 10 minutes to cool before removing it from the loaf pan.
8. Combine the butter, powdered sugar, vanilla, and milk in a medium mixing bowl. Swirl over the bread.

22. LEMON POPPY SEED BREAD

Prep Time: 05 mins

Cook Time: 40 mins

Ingredients

- 2 cups of sugar
- 4 cups of flour
- 2 tbsp baking powder
- 1 tsp salt
- 2 eggs
- 2 cups of milk
- 2/3 cup of vegetable oil
- 2 tbsp lemon extract
- 1 tbsp lemon zest about the zest of 1 lemon
- 1 1/2 tbsp poppy seeds

Instructions

1. Heat the oven and grease 6 miniature loaf pans to 350 degrees.
2. In a medium mixing bowl, add the sugar, flour, baking powder and salt. Only set aside.
3. Combine the eggs, milk, oil, lemon extract, and zest in a separate mixing bowl.
4. Poppy seeds fold in.
5. Upon wetting, steadily substitute the dry mixture until just damp.
6. To make up for the rise, dump flour into loaf pans an inch below.
7. Bake for 40 minutes. Enable 10 minutes to cool before removing it from the loaf pan.

Cook's Note

I. Milk-Milk brings sweetness to fast bread and gives them a beautiful brown color thanks to milk and sugar caramelization! From skim to vitamin D, you can use whatever you have on hand, including almond milk, to make it milk-free.

II. Vegetable Oil- This bread is extremely moist with vegetable oil. You may use canola oil, melted butter, or melted coconut oil as a supplement.

III. Lemon Extract brings a bright taste to this delicious bread! You should replace it with 4 teaspoons of lemon zest.

IV. Lemon Zest-Incorporates texture, color, and taste. You should substitute 1 1/2 tsp of extra lemon extract for this.

1. VEGETABLE BANANA SPLIT

Prep Time: 40 mins

Cook Time: 40 mins

Servings: 04

Ingredients

Mashed Potatoes:

- 2 pounds peeled and cubed russet potatoes
- 3 tbsp butter
- 1/2 Cup of milk
- Salt and pepper
- Barbecue sauce
- 3 tbsp butter
- 2 tbsp flour
- 1 tbsp paprika
- 1 tbsp dry mustard
- 2 Cup of chicken broth
- 1/4 Cup of chili sauce
- 1 tbsp Worcestershire sauce

Fried Bananas:

- 2 peeled green bananas
- 1 Cup of vegetable oil

Garnish:

- 4 cherry tomatoes
- Crushed roasted peanuts as need
- Sour cream

Instructions

Mashed potatoes:

1. In medium pressure, boil the potatoes in salted water until tender, about 15 minutes. Drain. Drain.
2. Using an electric mixer, purée the butter and milk until smooth. Seasoning change.
3. Keep wet.

Barbecue Sauce:

1. Melt butter in a medium-heat saucepan. Add the flour, stirring continuously until the mixture starts to brown, around 3 minutes.
2. Drop paprika and dry mustard. Add the broth and simmer while stirring with whisk. Add the remaining ingredients, reduce heat, cook until thickened, around 10 minutes. Set aside.

Fried Bananas:

1. Line a paper towel cookie sheet. Set aside.
2. Cut bananas halfway lengthwise.
3. With adult guidance, heat oil over medium-high heat in a large saucepan or deep skillet. Fry bananas yellow on both ends. Drain well on towels.

Assembly:

1. Serve in cut banana bowls.
2. Using an ice scoop, place 3 mashed potato scoops in each bowl. Drizzle with sauce, placed half a fried banana in each bowl.
3. Garnish with cherry tomato and sour cream dollop. Sprinkle peanuts. Serve with Chicken BBQ.

2. CHOCOLATE PEANUT CLUSTERS

Prep Time: 05 mins

Cook Time: 10 mins

Total Time: 15 mins

Ingredients

- 2 pounds white chocolate melts
- 21 ounces semisweet chocolate chips
- 14 ounces milk chocolate chips
- 13 ounces unsalted peanuts
- 13 ounces salted peanuts

Instructions

✓ Line 1-2 large parchment-paper sheets.

Stove Top:

1. Throw the chocolate in a heavy pot or pan over low heat.
2. Cook sometimes until melted and smooth. Cool 5 minutes, then stir in nuts.
3. Using a cookie scoop or metal spoon to lower the mixture on prepared baking sheets. Refrigerate to set.

Slow Cooker:

1. Spray a slow cooker tank with nonstick oil spray.
2. In all ingredients, cover and cook for 1-2 Hrs or until chocolate is fully melted.
3. Offer the mixture to blend.
4. Using a cookie scoop or metal spoon to lower the mixture on prepared baking sheets. Refrigerate to set.

Cook's Note

Refrigerate in a freezer or freeze until 2 months.

Nutrition Facts

Calories: 243kcal | Carbohydrates: 21g | Protein: 4g | Fat: 16g | Cholesterol: 4mg | Sodium: 46mg | Potassium: 187mg | Fiber: 2g | Sugar: 16g | Calcium: 53mg | Iron: 1mg

3. CHOCOLATE PEANUT BUTTER BALLS

Prep Time: 35 mins

Cook Time: 05 mins

Total Time: 40 mins

Ingredients

- 1/2 Cup of creamy peanut butter
- 3 tbsp softened salted butter
- 1 Cup of powdered sugar
- 8 ounces semi-sweet chopped chocolate

Instructions

1. Mix butter and peanut in a measuring bowl. Gradually stir in powdered sugar until well in a dough ball. If required, add more powdered sugar at a time before the mixture stays together in a big ball.
2. Cover and let peanut butter dough sit for 15 minutes or firmly cover with plastic wrap and refrigerate until ready to form balls.
3. Shape into 1-inch balls, place on a baking sheet, cover and refrigerate for at least 20 minutes. Dough balls should form before dipping into chocolate. Add refrigeration time if necessary.
4. Melt chocolate with box instructions.
5. Dip peanut butter balls into molten chocolate, allowing excess dripping. Place on waxed baking sheet, cover and refrigerate until ready to eat.

Cook's Note

The peanut butter dough can be made, firmly wrapped in plastic, and cooled for a few days before ready to form balls. Once peanut butter balls are shaped, they can also be refrigerated in plastic wrap until ready to dip in chocolate.

4. CHOCOLATE SOUFFLE

Prep Time: 30 mins

Cook Time: 50 mins

Servings: 06

Ingredients

- Unsalted butter for baking dish
- 1/4 Cup of sugar
- 8 ounces finely chopped semisweet chocolate
- 1 tsp pure vanilla extract
- 3 large egg yolks, lightly beaten + 4 large egg whites
- 1/4 tsp cream of tartar

Instructions

1. Heat the oven to 350F. Lightly butter a 1 1/2-quarter bakery. Coat with sugar, overlapping. Set dish on a baking sheet.
2. Combine chocolate, vanilla & 1/4 cup water in a large, heat-proof bowl set over a skillet. Mix smoothly until melts, about 10 minutes. Remove from heat, cool 20 minutes.
3. Stir egg yolks in chocolate mixture until well mixed. Set aside souffle platform.
4. Beat egg whites and tartar cream in a wide bowl until soft peaks form, around 2 minutes, using an electric mixer. Add sugar & beat until stiff, glossy peaks, about 5 minutes.
5. In two additions, fold the egg-white mixture into the base of the souffle: with a rubber spatula, carefully cut through the middle and raise some base from the bowl. Turning bowl, starting to cut and lift base slowly until combined.
6. Transfer mixture to dish, stop having batter on top of the dish: smooth top. Bake until puffed and set, 30-35 minutes. Immediately serve.

5. VANILLA CHEESECAKE

Prep Time: 10 mins

Cook Time: 01 Hr 5 mins

Total Time: 01 Hr 15 mins

Ingredients

- 9-inch graham cracker crust
- 1 Cup of granulated sugar
- 8-ounce packages cream cheese
- 4 large eggs
- 2 tsp pure vanilla extract
- ⅓ Cup of heavy cream

For the Topping:

- Homemade Blueberry Sauce

Instructions

1. Heat the oven to 350°F. Carry a kettle of water to the bath.
2. Beat cream cheese and sugar for around 2 minutes in a stand mixer bowl fitted with paddle attachment, or in a wide bowl with electric mixer. Scrape the bowl sides and combine for another 30 seconds.
3. Add chickens, one by one, scratching the bowl sides after adding the second and fourth eggs. After inserting the final egg and scraping bowl sides, combine again for 30 seconds. Smooth and creamy the blend. Add vanilla and heavy cream and blend for 30 seconds.
4. Pour the cheesecake over packed crust.
5. Place the pan in a wider pan and pump boiling water halfway up the pan. Lay a sheet of foil carefully over the pan – don't tighten the foil, as we want air to circulate.
6. Bake the edges 55-65 minutes, but the middle will still have some jiggle. Turn off the oven, smash the handle. Enable one Hr oven cheesecake.
7. After 1 Hr, cut the cheesecake and place on a cooling rack to cool fully. When fully cooled, place it in the refrigerator for at least 8 Hrs.
8. Right before serving, top with homemade blueberry sauce.

Nutrition Facts

Calories 383, Total Fat 30g, Cholesterol 146mg, Sodium 269mg, Carbohydrates 22g, Fiber 0g, Sugar 20g, Protein 7g

6. BLACKBERRY VANILLA CHEESECAKE

Prep Time: 40 mins

Cook Time: 45 mins

Total Time: 01 Hr 25 mins

Ingredients

Cookie Crust:

- 1 Cup of Cookie crumbs
- 3 TBS Light Brown Sugar
- 1/2 tsp Cinnamon
- pinch salt
- 4 tbs melted unsalted butter

Vanilla Cheesecake:

- 3 pkg Full fat cream cheese
- 1 Cup of Sugar
- 2 tbs Cornstarch
- 1 Cup of Full Fat sour cream
- 3 Large Eggs
- 2 tsp Vanilla extract
- Zest of 1/2 an orange
- Pinch salt
- 2 Cup of Fresh blackberries

Instructions

To Make the Crust:

1. Mix cookies, sugar, salt, cinnamon, and melted butter in a food processor.
2. Spread crumbs thinly and force into the pan. Using the fingertips or a spoon's back.
3. Baker for 12 mins in a 350F heated oven.
4. When cooled, wrap the sides of the pan with tin foil and parchment paper and place in a larger pan. The pan should be wide enough to allow about 2" space between each pan and deep enough to fill up the side of the pan with water.

Vanilla Cheese Cake:

1. Heat the oven to 325F.
2. Mix sugar and cornstarch in a bowl.
3. Using a paddle-fitted stand mixer, beat the cream cheese at medium speed for around 1 minute. Scrape the bowl sides and bottom until clean and lump-free. Occasionally scrape bowl sides and rim.
4. Mix the sugar and cornstarch until smooth. Scrape the bowl sides and rim.
5. Add sour cream, blend until smooth.
6. Mix the eggs one by one, waiting for each egg to thoroughly incorporate before inserting the next, scratching the sides after each addition.
7. Vanilla extract or paste of bean, salt and orange zest. Mix 30 seconds.
8. Pour the batter over the cookie crust. Bang the counter to expel batter air. Place the fresh blackberry in the batter.
9. Place the cake in a larger pan center and fill the pan with boiling water halfway up the cheesecake pan sides. Make sure the cake batter doesn't sprinkle.
10. Cover the pans with aluminum foil, poke 4-5 times to allow air to flee.
11. Bake 40-45 minutes or jiggle the cake core like jelly.
12. Turn off the oven and shut for 1-3 Hrs.
13. Take the cake from the oven and knife between the cake and the sides of the pan.

7. CHOCOLATE CUP OF CAKES

Prep Time: 15 mins

Cook Time: 15 mins

Servings:16

Ingredients

- 1 ⅓ Cup of all-purpose flour
- ¼ tsp baking soda
- 2 tsp baking powder
- ¾ Cup of unsweetened cocoa powder
- ⅛ tsp salt
- 3 tbsp softened butter
- 1 ½ Cup of white sugar
- 2 eggs
- ¾ tsp vanilla extract
- 1 Cup of milk

Instructions

1. Heat the oven to 350 . Line a paper or foil liner muffin. Sift flour, baking powder, cocoa and salt & baking soda.
2. Mix butter and sugar until light. Add eggs, beat well, add vanilla. Stir in the flour mixture: beat well. Fill 3/4 whole muffin cup.
3. Bake for 15 minutes in a heated oven, or until a toothpick is clean. Frost with your favorite cooling.

8. EGG FREE CUP OF CAKES

Prep Time: 10 mins

Cook Time: 19 mins

Additational Time: 05 mins

Ingredients

Egg-Free Vanilla cup of Cakes:

- 1 1/4 cup of all-purpose flour
- 1 cup of sugar
- 1 3/4 tsp baking powder
- 1/2 tsp salt
- 1/2 cup of whole milk
- 1/4 cup of vegetable oil
- 1/4 cup of apple sauce
- 1 tbsp vanilla extract or vanilla bean paste
- 1/2 cup of sour cream

Egg-Free Vanilla Buttercream:

- 1 cup of room temperature unsalted
- 1/2 tsp salt
- 1 1/2 tsp vanilla extract
- 3 1/2 cup of powdered sugar
- 1 tbsp heavy cream

Instructions

Egg Free Cup of Cakes:

1. Heat the oven to 350°F and cover the pans with cupcake liners.
2. Pour rice, sugar, baking powder and salt into a large bowl.
3. Whisk all milk, vegetable oil, apple sauce, vanilla extract, and sour cream in a separate bowl. Mix before the batter matches.
4. Fill 2/3 way full Cup of cake liners. Bake for 19 minutes, or until a few moist crumbs fall out.
5. Let the Cup of cakes cool for 5 minutes before moving to a cooling rack to finish cooling. To speed the cooling process, pop the pans into your freezer for about 30 minutes.

Egg Free Buttercream Frosting:

1. Beat the butter for 30 seconds with a paddle or whisk attachment, until smooth.
2. Mix the vanilla extract or bean paste and salt at low speed.
3. Add 1 cup at a time in powdered sugar. Alternate with hot cream splashes.
4. Mix before the ingredients are thoroughly combined and the desired consistency is achieved.
5. Add cream if dense frosting. Add more powdered sugar if thin.
6. Place the buttercream with your preferred frosting tip in a piping bag, and pipe broad swirls onto the fully cooled Cupcakes.
7. Garnish as needed, enjoy!

Cook's Note

Using an alternative dairy milk to supplement the whole milk and milk-free yogurt instead of the sour cream

To make an eggless gluten-free Cup of cakes, change into your own gluten-free flour blend for the AP flour this recipe demands and overmix the batter and let it rest for at least 30 minutes before baking for the best results.

9. KENTUCKY BUTTER CAKE

Prep Time: 20 mins

Cook Time: 1 Hr 15 mins

Total Time: 1 Hrs 35 mins

Yield: Serves: 12

Ingredients

- 1 Cup of butter
- 2 Cup of granulated sugar
- 4 eggs
- 1 tbsp vanilla
- 3 Cup of all-purpose flour
- 1 tsp kosher salt
- 1 tsp baking powder
- 1/2 tsp baking soda
- 1 Cup of buttermilk

Butter Glaze:

- 1/3 Cup of butter
- 3/4 Cup of granulated sugar
- 2 tbsp water
- 2 tsp vanilla

Instructions

1. Heat the oven to 325°F.
2. Grease a 10" butter pan or shorten rather liberally. Set aside the pan of flour.
3. Mix foods together in a bowl. Stir for 30 seconds, then add medium and stir for 3 minutes.
4. After boiling, let cool. Combine all components over a medium-low flame. Stir until butter melts, dissolving sugar. Don't carry simmer.
5. Using a knife to poke holes over the warm cake and spray the glaze thinly over the cake when in the pan.
6. Enable the cake to cool completely in the pan, then transform the cake into a serving tray.
7. Really, I like making this cake a day early, finding it more moist and tasty while it rests overnight.

10. THERMOMIX BUTTER CAKE

Prep Time: 10 mins

Cook Time: 35 mins

Servings: 01

Ingredients

- 160 g of softened butter
- 175 g of caster sugar
- 1 tsp vanilla extract
- 3 eggs
- 250 g of self raising flour
- 125 g of milk
- Pinch of salt

Instructions

1. Line the foundation and grease the sides of a 20cm tin and preheat the oven to 180 degrees.
2. Place butter and caster sugar in your Thermomix bowl, blend at speed 5 for 30 seconds. Scrape down the sides and mix at pace 4 for 20 seconds.
3. Add the eggs and 100g flour and blend at speed 4 for 10 seconds.
4. Blend ingredients together at high speed for 10 seconds or until smooth and fluffy.
5. Place the butter in the microwave, then bake it for 35 minutes
6. Cool 10 mins in the pan, then chill on a wire shelf.

11. CHERRY CLAFOUTIS

Prep Time: 15 mins

Yield: Serves: 06

Ingredients

- 2 cup of of fresh pitted sweet cherries
- 2 tbsp of blanched slivered almonds
- 3 eggs
- 1/2 cup of of sugar & 1 tbsp of brown sugar
- 1/2 cup of of all-purpose flour
- 1/8 tsp of salt
- 1 cup of of milk
- 3/4 tsp of almond extract
- 1 1/2 tsp of vanilla extract
- Powdered sugar for dusting

Instructions

1. Scatter with cherries and slivered almonds: Preheat the oven to 350°F. Butter and flour a 9X9 baking dish. Place the cherries in the dish.
2. Batter with eggs, butter, salt and flour: mix together until smooth. Whisk salt and flour to smooth.
3. Add cream, almond and vanilla extract. Whisk smoothly.
4. Pour batter over the cherries and slivered almonds.
5. Bake: Bake at 350°F for 35-45 minutes or until a tester inserted in the middle is clean. Check about halfway through the baking and with aluminum foil if the surface gets browned.
6. Remove from the oven to cool: placing it off the oven can wiggle a little that's natural. Place a cool wire rack. The clafoutis may have slightly puffed up and will deflate when cooling.
7. Powdered sugar dust: cool clawfoots with powdered sugar. Serve.

12. BREAD PUDDING WITH NUTMEG

Prep Time: 15 mins

Cook Time: 40 mins

Total Time: 55 mins

Ingredients

- 2 large room temperature eggs
- 2 Cup of whole milk
- 1/4 Cup of cubed butter
- 3/4 Cup of sugar
- 1/4 tsp salt
- 1 tsp ground cinnamon
- 1/2 tsp ground nutmeg
- 1 tsp vanilla extract
- 4 1/2 to 5 Cup of soft bread cubes
- 1/2 Cup of raisins

Vanilla Sauce:

- 1/3 Cup of sugar
- 2 tbsp cornstarch
- 1/4 tsp salt
- 1-2/3 Cup of cold water
- 3 tbsp butter
- 2 tsp vanilla extract
- 1/4 tsp ground nutmeg

Instructions

1. In a bowl, gently beat eggs. Combine milk and butter with sugar, cinnamon, spices and vanilla. Add cubes of bread and, if desired, raisins.
2. Add a well-grained 11x7-in. Bake bowl. Bake at 350° until inserted 1 in. From edge clean, 40-45 minutes.
3. Meanwhile, in a curry, combine sugar, cornstarch and salt. Remove before smooth. Cook over medium heat and whisk until thickened, around 2 minutes. Add the heat butter, vanilla, and nutmeg. Serve soft pudding.

13. BREAD AND BUTTER PUDDING

Prep Time: 10 mins

Cook Time: 25 mins

Total Time: 35 mins

Ingredients

- 8 heaped Cup of white bread, preferably slightly stale
- 1 Cup of sultanas

EGG MIXTURE:

- 3 eggs
- 1 1/2 Cup of milk
- 1 Cup of heavy or thickened cream
- 3 tbsp unsalted melted and cooled butter
- 1/2 Cup of white sugar
- 1 tsp cinnamon powder
- 1 tsp vanilla extract

FINISHES / SERVING:

- 2 tbsp unsalted melted butter
- Icing sugar or powdered sugar for dusting
- Ice cream, cream, custard, chocolate sauce and caramel sauce

Instructions

1. Heat the oven to 350°F.
2. Egg Mixture: Place eggs in a bowl, whisk briefly. Add remaining ingredients and whisk.
3. Soak Bread: Add bread and sultanas, combine and set aside for 3 minutes to allow egg mixture to soak through the bread.
4. Transfer to Baking Dish: Pour into a bakery. If you have several sultanas on the surface, poke them below the surface.
5. Drizzle then Bake: Drizzle over melted butter and bake for 25 - 30 minutes or until crispy on top, but still slightly wobbly inside.
6. Remaining 1 1/2 tbsp of melted butter, then icing sugar particles.
7. Serve - Rest for a couple minutes, then serve quickly, choose toppings! I want ice cream, custard and cream.

Cook's Note

Bread - While the classic version is made of plain white bread, you can do this for every option of bread including raisin bread, hot cross buns, brioche, everything!

14. OREO RICE KRISPY BARS

Prep Time: 20 mins

Cook Time: 06 mins

Cooling Time: 15 mins

Total Time: 41 mins

Ingredients

HOMEMADE MARSHMALLOW:

- 1/2 ounces unflavored gelatin powder
- 1 cup of divided water
- 1 cup of granulated sugar
- 1 cup of light corn syrup
- 1 tsp vanilla
- 1/8 tsp salt
- 4 tbsp melted and cooled butter

RICE KRISPY BAR:

- 4 cups of Rice Krispy cereal
- 1 package crumbled Oreo Cookies
- 2 cups of mini marshmallows

Instructions

1. Line a square, an 8-inch baking dish with parchment.
2. Combine the gelatin and 1/2 cup of water in an electric mixer bowl. The sugar mixture is formulated and the gelatin will bloom as you do this.
3. In a tiny saucepan, add 1/2 cup of water, sugar, and light corn syrup to a simmer.
4. Boil the pan until it exceeds 240 ° F
5. and extract it from the heat.
6. Using the mixer at a medium pace and using the whisk attachment, gently add the heated liquid onto the gelatin.
7. Increase the mixture to high speed and beat until it turns white and soft.

8. Add the salt, vanilla, and melted butter, and turn the mixer to medium. Enable for another min or so to mix on high, and then remove the bowl from the stand mixer.
9. Rice Krispies, crumbled Oreo Cookies, and mini marshmallows are thrown in and mixed by hand.
10. Until it is well-coated, this could take about a minute and a little elbow grease to stir.
11. Transfer the mixture to the baking dish which has been packed. Press the mixture down a bit, then scatter on top of the remaining Oreo. Using your hand to press the bars down so that they are all the same height.
12. To ensure the marshmallows are ready, refrigerate for 10-15 mins.
13. Serve and enjoy!

15. OREO FLUFF

Prep Time: 10 mins

Ingredients

- 8 ounces cream cheese, room temperature
- 14 ounces sweetened condensed milk
- 16 ounces whipped topping
- 16 roughly broken Oreos

Instructions

1. In a stand mixer, place cream cheese and sweetened condensed milk and blend for 1 min, on high.
2. Take the bowl from the blender and add in the whipped topping with your palm.
3. For the topping, add split Oreo's and swirl until integrated.
4. Chill until fed, or feed quickly.

16. OREO COOKIE DESSERT RECIPE

Prep Time: 20 mins

Cook Time: 20 mins

Ingredients

FOR THE CRUST:

- 1 box chocolate cake mix
- 1 whole egg + 3 egg yolks
- 1 tbsp butter

FOR THE TOPPING:

- 8 ounces softened cream cheese
- 1/2 cup of powdered sugar
- 1 tsp vanilla
- 2 small boxes, instant chocolate pudding
- 3 cups of milk
- 1 tub, 8 oz, whipped topping, thawed
- 10 crushed Oreo sandwich cookies

Instructions

FOR THE CRUST:

1. Heat the oven to 350. For frying, grease a 9x13 glass baking dish with nonstick oil.
2. In a mixing bowl, mix the cake batter, eggs, and butter. Mix by hand until it shapes a dough. Onto a prepared tub, press the dough.
3. Bake for 20 minutes or until fixed in the middle. Remove from of the oven and cool fully before topping.

FOR THE TOPPING:

1. Using a blender to blend cream cheese, powdered sugar, and vanilla. Smooth beat before. Spread the crust on top.
2. Place together the pudding and milk and whisk well. Pour on a sheet of cream cheese. For 10 mins, refrigerate.
3. Remove and cover with whipped icing and crushed cookies from the refrigerator. Immediately serve or refrigerate before ready to serve, protected.

17. NO BAKE PEANUT BUTTER OREO DESSERT

Prep Time: 15 mins

Total Time: 15 mins

Ingredients

- 20 peanut butter OREO sandwich cookies
- 1/4 cup of melted butter
- 4 oz softened and cubed cream cheese
- 1/2 cup of powdered sugar
- 1/4 cup of creamy peanut butter
- 1 tsp vanilla
- 1 package, Reese's mini peanut butter cups, halved

Instructions

1. Place cookies with OREO in a food processor. Process until you have fine crumbs for 20 seconds. Pour in the melted butter and pulse until well combined for 10 seconds.
2. With a removable rim, push into a round tart tray. Place it in the fridge.
3. Rinse the food processor bowl and blade and rinse it. Add the cream cheese, peanut butter, powdered sugar, and vanilla. The process once well combined. The sides of the bowl and procedure may need to be scraped off.
4. Remove the tart out of the fridge and spread the filling on top of the crust.
5. Cover them with cups of peanut butter.
6. Refrigerate before eating for at least an hour. Cut into 10-12 wedges and store in the fridge.

18. OREO CHEESECAKE BITES RECIPE

Prep & Cook Time: 10 mins + 50 mins

Yield: 06 Servings

Ingredients

Crust:

- 15 crumbled Oreo cookies
- 3 tbsps of melted butter

Filling:

- 1 package of cream cheese & 1 egg
- 8-10 crushed Oreos
- ¼ cup of sour cream
- 2 tbsps of flour
- ½ cup of melted chocolate for serving

Instructions

1. Heat the oven to 350 F. Set up a cup of foil on the cake tray.
2. For a crust, mix the Oreo crumbs with the melted butter. Scoop 1 1/2-2 tbsps. Each cup of cake mold is mixed and pressed as tightly and uniformly as possible. Bake for 10 minutes, then absolutely let cool.
3. Decrease the temperature to 320 F. Whisk together the cream cheese, rice, egg, and sour cream. To the batter, add crushed Oreos.
4. Load the batter into cups of cake molds and return for 40 more minutes to the oven.
5. Remove from the pan and drizzle with molten chocolate and let the cheesecake bites cool down.

19. NO-BAKE OREO CHEESECAKE RECIPE

Prep Time: 15 mins

Additional Time: 03 hours

Total Time: 03 hours 15 mins

Ingredients

- 1 Oreo pie crust
- 8 oz softened cream cheese
- 1/4 cup of granulated sugar
- 2 tsp vanilla extract
- 8 oz. whipped topping
- 10 crushed Oreo cookies

Instructions

1. Place the Oreo cookies in a big Ziploc bag and softly crush them into tiny pieces using a rolling pin, then set them aside.
2. Mix the cream cheese, sugar, and vanilla extract in a large bowl, until smooth.
3. Mix in the Oreo cookies that were chopped. Mixing cheesecake cookies
4. Fold in the whipped topping until you are careful not to beat or over mix the whipped topping until just mixed.
5. Spread the mixture onto the Oreo cookie crust that has been packed.
6. Before serving, cover and chill for at least 3 hours in the refrigerator.
7. Add extra whipped icing and cookies or cookie crumbs to the tip. Oreo cheesecake sandwich on a white tray

Cook's Note

Whipped topping versus whipped cream performs better using this formula. The stabilized whipped topping offers a stronger outcome and is retained when frozen and thawed.

20. AIR FRYER BISCUIT OREO COOKIES

Total Time: 10 mins

Servings: 08

Ingredients

- 1 can refrigerated biscuits
- 8 cream-filled chocolate sandwich cookies
- 2 tbsp powdered sugar

Instructions

1. Heat the Air Fryer with an Air Fryer pan to 375°.
2. Biscuits separately. Used a pin roller. Flatten one biscuit out. In the middle, place one cookie.
3. Fold the cookie with the biscuit around it. From side - to - side and from top to bottom thereafter. I folded mine and then pinched the closed corners.
4. Place the biscuit and close it in the middle of your Air Fryer pan. Cook for 2-3 mins at 375 °, or until golden brown.
5. Turn over and cook for until golden brown. The Cook Times could differ.
6. Sprinkle with sugar powder and serve warmly.

21. SLUTTY PUMPKIN CHEESECAKE BARS

Prep Time: 25 mins

Cook Time: 01 hr 15 mins

Total Time: 01 hr 40 mins

Ingredients

Brownie:

- 1 box milk chocolate brownie mix
- 3 large eggs
- ¼ Cup water
- ½ Cup canola oil
- 1 package Halloween Oreos
- ½ Cup mini chocolate chips

Pumpkin Cheesecake:

- 12 oz softened cream cheese
- ⅔ Cup pumpkin puree
- ⅔ Cup sugar
- 2 large eggs
- 1 tsp pure vanilla extract
- 1 tsp pumpkin pie spice
- ⅛ tsp kosher salt

Instructions

1. Heat the oven to 350F. Line a 9x9 baking pan with parchment paper.
2. Whip all the brownie ingredients together using a large bowl and hand mixer.
3. Load the flour into the dish to roast.
4. Cover with a sheet of the whole Oreos on the brownie batter.
5. Only set aside.
6. Beat together the cream cheese, pumpkin puree, butter, vanilla, pumpkin pie spice, and salt until mixed and smooth, using another large mixing bowl.
7. Beat the eggs until mixed and creamy, 1 at a time.
8. Pour over the brownie batter with the cheesecake batter.
9. Chop up between 5-8 cookies of oreo and scatter with the cheesecake batter on top.
10. Sprinkle on top of 1/2 C of small chocolate chips.
11. Bake for around 75 mins in the oven or until the middle is set and the sides begin to peel away from the paper of the parchment.
12. Enable it to cool to room temperature before cooling overnight in the refrigerator.
13. Cut into bars to enjoy!

22. MAGIC OREO BARS

Prep Time: 05 mins

Cook Time: 30 mins

Yield: 24 Servings

Ingredients

- 1/2 cup of melted butter
- 1 1/2 cups of Oreo crumbs
- 14 ounces sweetened condensed milk
- 1 cup of semisweet chocolate chips
- 1 cup of white chocolate chips
- 20 quartered Oreos
- 1 1/3 cups of flaked coconut

Instructions

1. Heat the oven to 350 degrees. Cover a baking pan 13 x 9 inches with baking oil.
2. Place the Oreo crumbs and butter together.
3. Press the prepared pan to the bottom.
4. Pour the sweetened condensed milk generously over the mixture of crumbs.
5. Layer uniformly with chocolate chips, white chocolate chips, almond, and quartered Oreos.
6. For a fork, press down hard.
7. Bake for 30 minutes or until browned gently.
8. Before slicing, let the bars cool before.

Nutrition Facts

Calories: 296g, Carbohydrates: 33g, Protein: 4g, Fat: 18g, Cholesterol: 18mg, Sodium: 156mg, Potassium: 194mg, Fiber: 2g, Sugar: 25g, Calcium: 73g, Iron: 2g

23. PEANUT BUTTER OREO BARS

Yield: 24 Servings

Prep Time: 20 mins

Total Time: 02 hours 20mins

Ingredients

Oreo Layer:

- 2 tbsp melted unsalted butter
- 14 Oreos

Peanut Layer:

- 1/2 cup of melted unsalted butter
- 1 cups of graham cracker crumbs
- 1 cups of powdered sugar
- 1/2 cup of peanut butter

Chocolate Layer:

- 4 tbsp peanut butter
- Semisweet chocolate chips
- , 1 1/2 cups

Instructions

1. In a mixing bowl, add Chocolate bars and process it until fine crumbs are formed.
2. Mix the butter and Oreos and press them uniformly into the 8x8 baking pan and freeze for 10 minutes.
3. In a stand mixer, add the sugar, peanut butter, and graham cracker crumbs until smooth, about 1 min.
4. Add the powdered sugar until well mixed and smooth, around 2 mins, at the lowest speed level.
5. Spread the peanut butter filling uniformly into the baking dish and return to the freezer gently.
6. In a medium saucepan over medium pressure, incorporate the peanut butter and chocolate chips.
7. Constantly stir until creamy, then spill over the layer of peanut butter and tilt to scatter.
8. Refrigerate before slicing for at least 2 hours.
9. Serve and enjoy!

24. OREO CHEESECAKE COOKIE

Prep Time: 01 hours 30 mins

Cook Time: 10 mins

Total Time: 01 hours 40 mins

Ingredients

Chocolate Cookie:

- 2 cups of all-purpose flour
- 1/4 cup of Dutch-processed cocoa powder sifted
- 1/4 cup of black cocoa powder sifted
- 1 tsp baking soda
- 1/2 tsp salt
- 1 cup of unsalted butter
- 1/2 cup of granulated sugar
- 1 cup of light brown sugar packed
- 2 large eggs room temperature
- 1 tsp vanilla

Oreo Cheesecake Filling:

- 1 cup of heavy whipping cream chilled
- 8 oz cream cheese full fat, softened
- 1/2 cup of granulated sugar
- 3/4 cup of Oreo cookie crumbs

Instructions

Chocolate Cookie:

1. Heat the oven to 350°. With cooking oil, spray two standard-sized muffin tins.
2. Whisk the rice, cocoa powder, baking soda, and salt together. Only set aside.
3. On med-high, beat the butter and sugar until light and fluffy. Reduce the rpm and add vanilla and eggs one at a time. Beat before they're mixed. Add the combination of flour and blend until just mixed.
4. Press down to flatten a large cookie scoop scoop dough into muffin tins.
5. Bake until approx. 10-13mins or until almost set, in the center, but still soft.

6. Remove it from the oven and use a small jar or tub instantly to press tightly down in the middle to create a well. Cool for 10mins in pans. Loosen each by turning it in the pan slightly. Remove from the pan and cool absolutely on a wire rack for 5 more minutes.

Oreo Cheesecake Filling:

1. Whip the heavy cream until its peaks are stiff. Beat the cream cheese and sugar in a separate bowl until soft. Add and pound Oreo cookie crumbs before integrated.
2. Add whipped cream to the combination of cream cheese and stir until mixed.
3. Pipe and refrigerate in cooled cookie cups until set. When needed, sprinkle with extra Oreo cookie crumbs.
4. Serve and eat chilled within 2-3 days.

25. COOKIES 'N CREAM OREO CAKE ROLL

Prep Time: 48 mins

Cook Time: 12 mins

Yield: 12 Slice

Ingredients

FOR THE CAKE:

- 3 large eggs
- Unsweetened dark cocoa powder, 1/4 cup
- 3/4 cup of granulated sugar
- 2 tsp brewed coffee
- 1 tsp vanilla extract
- 1/4 tsp salt
- 1 tsp baking powder
- 3/4 cup of all-purpose flour
- Powdered sugar to aid in rolling

FOR THE FILLING:

- 3/4 cups of heavy whipping cream
- 1 tbsp powdered sugar
- 1 tsp vanilla extract
- 12 Oreos crushed

Instructions

1. Cake Making: Heat the oven to 350 degree F. Using foil to line a jelly roll pan and cover with cooking spray.
2. Beat the eggs for 3 mins at high speed, before they are frothy and dark yellow. Beat in the vanilla powder, coffee or water, and honey.
3. Whisk the chocolate, cinnamon, baking powder, and flour together. Only whisk in the wet ingredients when mixed.
4. Spread in a ready-made pan. The flour would be in a slim layer and you should utilize a wooden spoon or spatula to spread it to all the edges of the plate. For 10-15 mins, bake. You'll know it's finished, and it will slightly bounce back if you softly prod the top with your fingertip.
5. Set up a clean kitchen towel before baking the cake in a large work room. Sprinkle white sugar liberally. Turn it over on a kitchen towel sprinkled with powdered sugar as soon as the cake comes out of the oven. Carefully cut the foil.
6. Fold over the cake with the side of the towel, working on the short end. Tightly roll and roll the cake onto the towel. Let cool absolutely for at least one hour when rolling.
7. Make the filling: beat strong whipping cream fitted with the whisk attachment in an electric mixer. When beating, slowly add powdered sugar and vanilla. Beat until it shapes whipped cream. Stir in crushed Oreos, reserving to garnish a tbsp or two.
8. Assemble Cake: Unroll it slowly until the cake has cooled. On the cake, spread the whipped cream, leaving 1" at each end without filling. Re-roll the cake and spoon out any filling that spills out when you roll. Before frosting, cover with plastic wrap and chill for at least one hour. You can use it for topping if you have leftover whipped cream, or top it up as I did, see next step.
9. Make the topping: In a microwave-safe mixing cup or bowl, place chocolate chips and strong whipping cream. Heat for 60-90 seconds on high power or until the cream is hot, then whisk until smooth. For 10 mins, let it cool.
10. Place the roll of cake on a wire rack spread over a cookie sheet. Pour the ganache uniformly over the cake. Cover of smashed cookies leftover. Until ready, chill.

Cook's Note

Before just before eating, the cake should remain chilled, or the whipped cream filling will get warm, and it will be difficult to slice.

CONCLUSION

An air fryer oven is an outstanding appliance for maintaining your diet. If you prefer deep-fried food, you can still enjoy its flavor without ingesting high amounts of fat.

Air fryer is a must-have item in any kitchen, domestic or commercial. Customers switch to the flexibility and health advantages this modern wave of cooking appliances provides.

---Thank You Very Much---

Printed in Great Britain
by Amazon